The Prophets
Speaking Out for Justice

Gila Gevirtz

Introduction by Rabbi Mark Levine

Behrman House Publishers

www.behrmanhouse.com
www.thejewishprophets.com

For Suri—my sister, my friend, my teacher.

—G.G.

Book and Cover Design: Terry Taylor Studio
Cartographer: Jim McMahon
Project Manager: Vicki L. Weber

The publisher gratefully acknowledges the cooperation of the following sources for photographs and graphic images: Bettmann/Corbis:54; Archana Bhartia/123.rf: 93; Samuel Cohen/Adiv Photography: 53; P.J. Cross/Shutterstock: cover, 6; Culver Pictures, Inc./Superstock: 70; Andy Dean/123.rf: 88; Gustave Dore:1, 3, 4, 7, 10, 11, 18, 19, 22, 23, 25, 32, 36, 37, 38, 48, 49, 50, 60, 61, 68, 72, 73, 80, 84, 85, 89, cover; Gila Gevirtz: 39;The Granger Collection: 13; Greater New York Conference on Soviet Jewry; 83; Kevin D. Hendricks/Startseeingart.com: 54; Imagesource:/123.rf: 17; Hanan Isachar/Superstock: 31; Javarman/123.rf: 94; Terry Kaye: 4, 45; Jerry Lampen/Reuters Corbis: 35; Lebrecht Photo Library: 77; Eric Lessing/Art Resources: 29; Richard Lobell: 12, 24, 43, 46, 82; Joseph Muellek: 20; G. Dagli Orti/Art Resources: 27; Joseas Reys/123.rf: 69; Stockxpert: 57; The Helen Suzman Foundation: 21; Temple Aaron, St. Paul: 54; Ginny Twersky: 58; Vicki Weber: 46, 65, 74; Ned White/123.rf: 65; World Wide Photos 95; Lisa Young/123.rf: 90.

Published by Behrman House, Inc.
Springfield, NJ 07081
www.behrmanhouse.com

ISBN: 978-0-87441-600-8
Manufactured in the United States

Library of Congress Cataloging-in-Publication Data
Gevirtz, Gila.
        The prophets speaking out for justice/Gila Gevirtz; introduction by Mark Levine.
            p. cm.
        ISBN 978-0-87441-600-8
Bible. O.T. Prophets- - Criticism, interpretation, etc. 2. Justice. 3. Jewish ethics
Title.
BS1505.52.G48 2010
224'.08303372- -dc22   2010006684

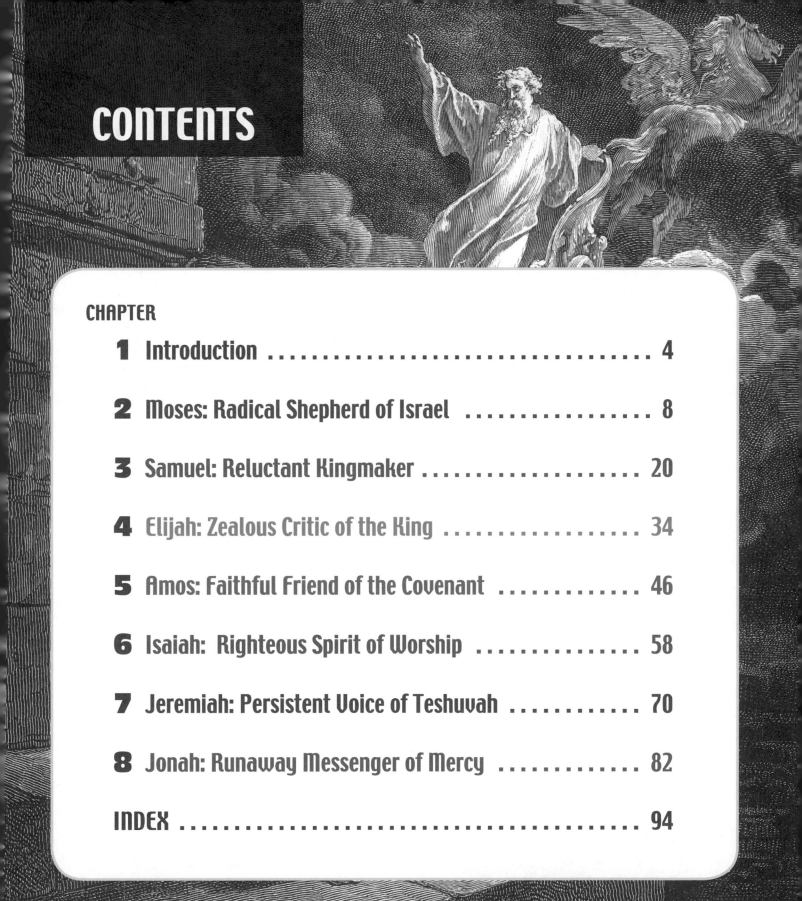

CONTENTS

CHAPTER 1 Introduction

Immediately after reading the Torah on Shabbat and holiday mornings, Jews in synagogues around the world listen as a congregant chants (or reads) the *Haftarah*—a selection excerpted from the section of the Bible known as *Nevi'im*, Prophets. This ritual, which you will perform for the first time when you become a bar or bat mitzvah, originated two thousand years ago, but its beginnings are shrouded in mystery. One theory suggests that the practice of reading a *Haftarah* portion arose in response to religious persecution by Antiochus Epiphanes, the Syrian-Greek emperor whose anti-Jewish edicts led to the Maccabee revolt in 167 BCE. (We celebrate the success of that rebellion during Hanukkah.) But before resorting to armed resistance, Jewish authorities waged a battle of deception against their occupiers. When Antiochus outlawed reading the Torah in public, communal leaders substituted readings from the lesser known books of the prophets. To maintain a clandestine connection to the weekly Torah readings, they chose portions that related to the theme or narrative of each Torah reading. Their imaginative ploy worked, and Greek officials unknowingly allowed religious study to continue.

This explanation prompts an interesting question: Why has the practice of reading a message from the prophets on Shabbat and holidays continued long after the ruse was no longer needed? To help us answer, we must understand more about the lives of the prophets and the meaning and significance of their messages. This book will guide our exploration.

Before we meet the prophets, let's consider a few terms.

Prophecy (n'vu'ah) – Think of prophecy as God's method of communicating with the Jewish people. You might immediately imagine the burning bush aflame or Mt. Sinai quaking violently. Our sacred texts describe natural spectacles like these at moments of human contact with the Divine, but these displays are not God's message. Prophecy comes in "a still, small voice" (1 Kings 19:12). At the foot of Mt. Sinai, however, that voice seemed terrifying, so the Israelites pleaded with Moses to intercede, saying, "You go closer and hear all that God says, then tell us everything and we will do it" (Deuteronomy 5:24). The model of the prophetic process was established; thereafter, God would only call upon individuals to carry divine messages to the people. The chosen individual is called a *navi*, a word that entered Hebrew from an ancient Mesopotamian language and which originally meant "one who has been called." Moses is considered the greatest prophet of the Jewish people, so it is fitting that this book begins with him.

Prophet (navi) – The prophets were God's mouthpiece. Once called to speak on God's behalf, they had no choice but to obey. Amos, a prophet from the eighth century BCE whom you will meet in chapter five,

As you prepare for your bat or bar mitzvah, you can remember that whenever you chant the *Haftarah*, you share in taking this ancient practice into the next generation of Jews around the world.

From their own time and into ours, the prophets lead others toward ethical values that have sustained Judaism for centuries.

described his helplessness: "A lion has roared, who can but fear? My God has spoken, who can but prophesy?" (Amos 3:8).

Although the prophets lacked free will to resist God's call, they maintained creative freedom in how they communicated God's message. For example, wails and laments characterized Isaiah's style (he even went naked for three years; you'll meet Isaiah, albeit with his clothes on, in chapter six), while Jeremiah (who is introduced in chapter seven) developed an angry, ranting style. Today, we use the word "jeremiad" to describe a prolonged, angry harangue, like many that poured out of Jeremiah. Regardless of their individual prophetic styles, all the prophets were courageous; they needed to be because the messages they delivered often rebuked people's behavior.

The prophet's message *(divrei n'vi'ut)* – *Nevi'im* is divided into two parts: Early Prophets and Later Prophets. The later prophets introduced in this book are Amos, Isaiah, Jeremiah, and Jonah. They are considered literary prophets because they wrote down their prophecies. The early prophets you'll meet in these pages are Samuel and Elijah. Like other prophets in this category, they never wrote about their lives and prophecies but, instead, they appear in books that are primarily about Israel's history.

All around you there are teenagers as well as adults who walk in the footsteps of the prophets. You can look in your own family, school, and town. You can also find examples at www.thejewishprophets.com.

The main difference between the early and late prophets, though, is their message. The early prophets directed most of their energy toward centralizing the religious authority of the nation against pagan practices of the surrounding peoples. In contrast, the later prophets lived during times when the national religion was firmly established but faced external threats. Their message focused on the people's moral lapses, which the prophets believed threatened the nation's existence. Invading empires like Babylonia were God's instruments, punishing the people for their immorality. If Israel would return to the ways of justice and compassion, then their enemies would be subdued. The prophetic ideal of building a just society, which weaves its way through many *Haftarah* portions, has inspired Jews for centuries. Hearing this message each week not only links us to the great prophets of our tradition, it also motivates us to work toward fulfilling their sacred vision.

Fortunately, we're not dependent on ancient history to inspire us to pursue justice. Many courageous people, like Supreme Court Justice Ruth Bader Ginsburg and others you will find in this book and at www.thejewishprophets.com, walk in the prophets' footsteps. They have spent their lives speaking truth to power, defending the poor, and helping the most vulnerable among us. You'll find vignettes of several contemporary prophets in this book. Their inspiring stories remind us that the work of creating a better society remains unfinished. From their example, we learn that God's voice speaks through us when we stand up to injustice.

THE AGE OF PROPHECY

The Sages of the Talmud teach that the age of prophecy began with Moses in the thirteenth century BCE and ended with Malachi in the fifth century BCE. According to this perspective, when Malachi died, the Divine spirit departed Israel and God's will was no longer accessible to human beings.

There is an alternative view, however, and it asserts that the age of prophecy continues, even in our own time. For those who hold this idea, God is less like a parent controlling the human family from above, and more like a force in the universe that stirs the human heart and awakens us to act righteously. The biblical prophets, from this perspective, were inspired personalities who felt a keen moral responsibility to bring godlike behavior into the world. We too can hear the divine call that summons us to become God's partners, working toward improving the human condition and building a better society.

How will the lives of the prophets inspire YOU to speak out in the name of justice?

CHAPTER 2 Moses:
Radical Shepherd of Israel

The shepherd did as he was told. Slipping off his sandals, he stood barefoot on the sacred ground of Mount Horeb. Sparks encircled the blazing bush before him—a bush that burned yet was not consumed.

Adonai called out from the blaze, "I have seen the oppression and suffering of My people in Egypt, and I have heard their outcry. Therefore, I will send you to Pharaoh, and you will lead My people, the Israelites, out of Egypt."

Filled with awe, the man hid his face and stuttered, "Who am I to go before Pharaoh?...What shall I tell the Israelites?...What if they do not believe me?...I am slow of speech."

—based on Exodus 3–4

PROPHET'S PROFILE: MOSES

BEGINNINGS:

- Israelite born into slavery in ancient Egypt.

- Hebrew Name: Moshe, from the word meaning "draw." This name was inspired by the name Pharaoh's daughter gave Moses when she "drew him from the water." (Exodus 2:10)

PERSONAL:

- Father: Amram of the tribe of Levi; mother: Yocheved; siblings: Aaron and Miriam.

- Raised by: His mother and Pharaoh's daughter, princess of Egypt.

- Wife: Zipporah, daughter of Jethro; sons: Gershom and Eliezer.

- Led the Israelites out of slavery.

- Was the prophet through whom the Israelites received the Torah.

POSTS: LOAD

Who was Moses?

Favorite Site: Mount Sinai (BTW: Many scholars believe that Mount Horeb is another name for Mount Sinai.).

Favorite Holiday: Passover (Yup! Check out Exodus 12, the first Passover seder was in Egypt—complete with matzah and bitter herbs.).

Greatest Disappointment: Didn't make it to the Land of Israel, Eretz Yisrael.

Favorite Quotation: "You shall have no other gods besides Me" (Exodus 20:3).

Major Contribution: Taught the Israelites how to live in a godly way through sacred rituals and ethical behavior.

Go To   http://www.TheJewishProphets.com ▼

MOSES AND THE STRAY LAMB

The ancient rabbis tell a midrash that explains why God chose Moses as a prophet.

"Moses was tending his father-in-law's flock" (Exodus 3:1). Spotting a lamb that had scampered away, he ran after it and found the lamb drinking from a small pool of water. "I didn't know that you were thirsty," said Moses. "You must be tired." With that, the shepherd hoisted the lamb onto his shoulders and carried him back to the flock.

Witnessing this, God said, "Because you showed compassion in caring for your flock, you shall become the shepherd of Israel, the flock that is Mine."

—Exodus Rabbah 2:2

Exodus 15:20 teaches that Miriam was a prophet and a source of strength to our people. On Passover, some families place Miriam's cup next to Elijah's cup on their seder table. It is filled with spring water to remind us of the legend of Miriam's well, which teaches that wherever our ancestors wandered in the Sinai wilderness, Miriam's well appeared and sustained them, a sign of God's compassion.

Moses Discovers the Force of Justice and Compassion

As our tradition teaches, despite his hesitation, Moses followed God's command. But why? What were the Israelites to Moses? Sure, he was born to Israelite parents living in Egypt. But our sages tell us that he grew up in the Egyptian royal court, raised by the princess herself.

By the time Moses encountered God at the burning bush he had left Egypt, settled in Midian, and was living a comfortable life as a shepherd, married to a daughter of the Midianite priest Jethro. Why rock the boat? Why not walk away and forget the incident at Horeb? Forget the fire, the Voice, the Israelites.

The Torah doesn't describe what went through Moses's mind as he considered whether to accept God's command, but imagine what might have gone through yours. Having lived in Egypt and Midian for so many decades, surrounded by people who worshipped gods that were concerned with their own well-being and power, might the idea of God as devoted to people and their well-being seem odd or impossible?

Moses was surely awed and inspired as he considered what he had heard on Mount Horeb: The suffering of a slave people matters. The force of justice can overtake the might of oppression. Compassion can trigger actions that liberate a people.

These radical ideas not only spurred Moses to accept God's command, they also became the heart of his prophetic message and the ethical foundation of Judaism.

Models of Compassion

As an infant, Moses experienced the power of compassion. The Book of Exodus teaches that the midwives Shifrah and Puah saved his life when they defied Pharaoh's order to kill all Israelite boys at birth. Moses's mother placed him in a basket of reeds on the bank of the River Nile then told Moses's sister to watch over him that no harm might come to him. Spotting him among the reeds, Pharaoh's daughter drew him forth from the water and raised him as her son.

Each woman could have chosen to walk away from Moses. It surely would have been easier and less risky. But their compassion moved them to respond with kindness.

The rabbis tell a midrash that God rewarded Pharaoh's daughter for her compassion by naming her Bityah, meaning "God's daughter." What lessons do you think the rabbis wanted to teach?

_____

_____

STICKY STUFF

Compassionate acts, like other acts of kindness, can be sticky. One friend shows compassion to another by listening as the friend talks about her parents' divorce. Talking about it makes the girl feel better. Now the goodness of compassion is stuck in her heart and mind, so when she notices a classmate having difficulty with a math assignment, she gently asks him if she can be of help.

Describe a time when someone said or did something that showed compassion for you. How did it affect your mood and behavior?

_____

_____

Describe a time when you treated someone with compassion. How do you think the person felt? How did you feel?

_____

_____

Who Is Like God?

To celebrate their liberation from Egypt, the Israelites joined Moses in a song of praise for God. We continue to sing their song at synagogue services to this day: Mi Chamochah, "Who is like You, Adonai, among the heavenly? Who is like You, majestic in holiness, Awesome One of splendor, Doer of wonders?" (Exodus 15:11).

A Prophet's Work Is Never Done

Having accepted God's mission, Moses quickly returned to Egypt, got the backing of the Israelites, confronted Pharaoh with God's demands and a series of ten plagues, then led the Israelites out of Egypt to safety.

Four hundred years of slavery and finally the Israelites were free! Yes, the Israelites were grateful…but not for long. Although their faith in God and in Moses's leadership had given them the courage to pull up stakes and flee Egypt, the Israelites could not yet maintain their faith.

In the coming days and weeks, each time a new challenge arose, such as finding food and water, many Israelites felt their faith evaporate like morning dew. Frustrated and scared, they longed for the certainty of life in Egypt. Bondage may have been harsh, but at least it was predictable. As slaves, they knew what was expected of them and what they could expect from Pharaoh. They were less sure about life as a free people living in the service to God.

The African-American spiritual "Let My People Go" begins, "When Israel was in Egypt's land, let My people go! Oppressed so hard they could not stand, let My people go!" And the refrain is, "Go down, Moses, way down in Egypt's land; tell old Pharaoh to let My people go!" How do you think the story of the Israelites' Exodus has inspired other peoples to resist oppression?

A Symbol of Freedom

Throughout history, the biblical story of the Israelites' Exodus from Egypt has been an inspiration for the liberation of oppressed peoples. In 1782, one proposal for the official seal of the United States illustrated the splitting of the Sea of Reeds and the escape of the Israelites.

Explain the meaning of Benjamin Franklin's motto, "Rebellion to tyrants is obedience to God."

_____

_____

What do you think of this motto? How difficult or easy is it to spot a tyrant in real life?

_____

_____

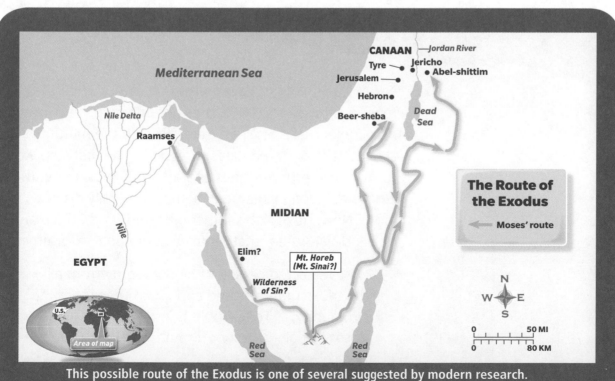

This possible route of the Exodus is one of several suggested by modern research. Some scholars think Mt. Horeb may be biblical Mt. Sinai.

The Israelites wandered in the parched wilderness of Shur for three days. Arriving in Marah, they found a stream but quickly spit out its bitter water grumbling, "Moses, what have you got for us to drink?"

Following God's instructions, Moses threw a piece of wood into the stream, and its waters became sweet. The people drank and continued on to Elim where they enjoyed the sweet water of twelve springs and the fruit of seventy palm trees. But by the time the caravan found its way to the wilderness of Sin, everyone's belly was empty again.

Seeing no sign of food or drink the former slaves wailed, "If only we had died in Egypt, where at least we had our fill of meat and bread. You have brought us to the wilderness to starve this whole community to death."

Even when the Israelites were given quail each evening and manna—honeyed wafers—under the morning dew, they continued to challenge Moses, asking, "Is Adonai present among us or not?"

—based on Exodus 15, 16, and 17

Lesser leaders might have stalked off or punished their rebellious followers. But Moses not only remained loyal to his people; he also helped them develop the maturity and skills to take on the duties of freedom. The first step was to share his responsibilities and authority with them. Moses alone had been in charge of settling the daily disputes that arose. Now, he took his father-in-law Jethro's advice and set up a judicial system that required communal involvement:

> Moses selected people of high integrity from all [the tribes of] Israel, and appointed them over the community…. They would bring the difficult cases to Moses but all the minor disputes they would judge themselves.
> —Exodus 18:25 – 26

By taking on responsibilities in the judicial system, the Israelites took their first step toward becoming a just people, learning to distinguish right from wrong and to work together so that their families and community could live in peace.

A Radical Idea Becomes a People's Reason for Being

Three months after the Israelites' Exodus from Egypt, Moses took another bold step. He had always had a larger prophetic vision than just leading the Israelites out of Egypt. He hadn't just demanded that Pharaoh let the Israelites go. He had told Pharaoh why. His message from God had been, "Let My people go *to serve Me*" (Exodus 9:1).

Now was the time to let the entire people share in the awe Moses had experienced on Mount Horeb. It was time to inspire them to accept the vision of God and the Covenant, or *Brit*, which would make God's just and compassionate laws their own.

What Do You Think?

What would it have been like if as soon as you could walk and talk you had been asked to earn a living? What are the benefits of receiving responsibility and authority gradually, in stages? What might make this frustrating?

How did Moses's action help the Israelites become a free and just people? When do you think he should have turned all the responsibility over to the people?

_____

_____

_____

Why might people who are confident that they will get their "piece of the pie"—enough food, warm clothing, and a safe home—be more patient and trusting than people who lack that confidence? What might be the challenges of leading people who are worried about their ability to survive?

His heart pounding, Moses summoned the elders of the community. Standing before them, he shared God's words: "You have seen what I did to the Egyptians, how I bore you on eagles' wings and brought you to Me. Now then, if you will obey Me faithfully and keep My covenant, you will be My treasured possession. You shall be to Me a kingdom of priests and a holy nation."

Without hesitation all the people answered as one saying, "Everything that Adonai has spoken we will do." They spoke for themselves and for every generation of Jews after them for all time, and Moses brought the people's words back to God.

—based on Exodus 19:4 – 8

The Covenant presented a radical vision of a god's relationship with humans. The Israelites had been invited into and accepted an eternal partnership with God. In addition, the status of being holy was extended to *all* the people—the entire nation of former slaves—not just to the prophet or a privileged class of religious leaders.

"Everything Adonai has spoken we will do."
Exodus 19:8

The Teachings

Having entered into the Covenant, the Israelites were now ready to receive the laws, or *mitzvot*, that would guide them as a holy people. Tradition teaches that the people gathered at the foot of Mount Sinai, and Moses went to the top of the mountain. When he returned, he repeated God's teachings, the Torah, to the people.

From the first commandments it became clear that God was concerned about people's everyday behavior—in relation to God and to one another. For an ancient people, this must have been shocking. Why would any god care about their everyday lives? What did it matter to the gods if people were just or unjust, honest or dishonest?

But the God of Moses did care, and to the God of Moses it did matter.

As God's prophet, Moses was asking the Israelites to accept a new idea: God would hold them accountable for performing acts of kindness, truth, and justice. To its credit, the newly liberated and imperfect nation was inspired by Moses's vision and accepted the challenge. It pledged to serve God and in return was promised God's protection.

Exodus 34:29 – 30 describes how, when Moses came down from Mount Sinai, he was carrying the stone tablets of the Ten Commandments. Light radiated from Moses's face because he had spoken with God. What do you think the light symbolizes?

Lessons of Justice and Compassion

Moses taught the Israelites many lessons about justice and compassion. What do these three teachings tell you about Moses's understanding of God? What do they teach you about what it means to be a fair and caring person?

- "If you take your neighbor's clothing as a pledge [for a loan], return it to your neighbor before the sun goes down [and it becomes cold].... In what else shall your neighbor sleep? For if your neighbor cries out to Me, I will pay attention, for I am compassionate" (Exodus 22:25 – 26).

- "God seeks justice for the orphan and the widow, and cares for the stranger, providing the stranger with food and clothing. You, too, must show concern for the stranger, for you were strangers in the land of Egypt" (Deuteronomy 10:18 – 19).

- "You shall not insult the deaf or place a stumbling block before the blind..." (Leviticus 19:14).

Judaism teaches that it is a religious obligation to act with compassion; for example, when we see people in need of food. Yet Judaism does not require us to *feel* compassionate. Why do you think our religion emphasizes actions over feelings? Do you think feelings are more important, or do you think actions are?

Jewish tradition teaches that Moses launched the Jewish people on a journey that has lasted for more than three thousand years. He took a slave people who had been oppressed for centuries, led them out of slavery, inspired them to become a nation with a holy purpose, and then gave them a code of laws to live by. It is no wonder that the closing words of the Torah are, "Never again did a prophet arise in Israel like Moses, whom Adonai knew face to face" (Deuteronomy 34:10).

Helen Suzman

Helen Suzman

Helen Suzman (1917 – 2009) was born in the mining town of Germiston, South Africa. Her parents, Lithuanian Jewish immigrants, had come to South Africa to escape the oppression of Jews in Lithuania. Ironically, South Africa had an oppressive government policy of apartheid: racial segregation and discrimination against blacks.

In 1948, when the pro-apartheid National Party came to power, Suzman joined the moderate United Party and was elected to Parliament in 1953. Six years later, Suzman helped form the anti-apartheid Progressive Party.

For thirteen years, Suzman was the sole anti-apartheid member of Parliament. Once criticized by another member of Parliament for embarrassing South Africa abroad because of the questions she raised about the government's discriminatory policies, Suzman responded, "It is not my questions that embarrass South Africa—it is your answers."

As white opposition to apartheid grew, Suzman eventually was joined in Parliament by white, liberal colleagues. She retired from Parliament in 1989 but remained a political activist, helping to oversee South Africa's first democratic election in 1994.

Describe one way in which Suzman's role was similar to Moses's. Describe one way in which it was different.

Similar: _____

_____

Different: _____

_____

Go To http://www.TheJewishProphets.com ▼

CHAPTER **3** Samuel:
Reluctant Kingmaker

The teen lay soundly asleep in the temple at Shiloh. Thirteen years earlier he had been the answer to his mother's prayers. In this same temple, she had asked God for a son. When Samuel was born, she gratefully dedicated his life to the service of God and brought him to live at the temple with Eli the priest.

Now, as dawn was about to break, God called out. Samuel answered, "I'm coming," and quickly ran to Eli saying, "Here I am. You called me."

But the priest replied, "I didn't call you. Go back to sleep."

Twice more Samuel heard the Voice and shuttled back and forth between his bed and Eli's room. The third time, the aging priest understood and said, "Go lie down. If you are called, say, 'Speak, Adonai, for Your servant is listening.'"

The fourth time Samuel was awakened, he listened and was called to prophecy.

—based on 1 Samuel 1:9 – 3:10

PROPHET'S PROFILE: SAMUEL

BEGINNINGS:

- Born in Ramah, in the hill country of Ephraim, in the second half of the eleventh century BCE.

- Hebrew Name: Sh'muel, meaning "God has heard." Samuel's mother said she named her son Sh'muel because "I asked God for him [and was heard]" (1 Samuel 1:20).

PERSONAL:

- Father: Elkanah of the tribe of Ephraim; mother: Hannah; siblings: three brothers and two sisters. (DNS: 1 Samuel 2:21)

- Childhood: As a toddler, entered the service of God with Eli the priest at Shiloh, home of the Ark of the Covenant, about twenty miles northeast of Jerusalem.

POSTS:

 LOAD

Who was Samuel?

Claim to Fame: Was the first major prophet to preach inside the Land of Israel and the last of the Israelite judges.

Kings He Anointed: Anointed, or performed the ritual that empowered, Saul and David as the first Israelite kings.

Greatest Disappointment: Couldn't persuade the Israelites to rely on God rather than on a human king.

Favorite Quotation: "Above all you must honor and serve Adonai faithfully with all your heart; and consider how generously God has dealt with you. For if you continue in your wrongdoing, both you and your king will be swept away" (1 Samuel 12: 24 – 25).

MAJOR CONTRIBUTION
Established a rule of kings, a monarchy, based on loyalty to God's teachings.

Go To http://www.TheJewishProphets.com ▼

Samuel—Prophet, Priest, and Judge

The last thing Samuel had ever wanted to do was anoint a king. Why would he? He believed that God was the Ruler of Israel. Even so, Samuel anointed two kings in his life, first Saul then David. What follows is the story of why Samuel was reluctant to establish the kingship and how he ended up doing so anyway, all the while remaining faithful both to his principles and to his people.

When Samuel was called to prophecy the Israelites had no king or central government. Instead, they had a loose union made up of twelve tribes with local leaders. Each tribe was overseen by a judge, or chieftain, who governed, settled disputes, and led the local army. Religious leadership was provided by local priests and prophets. Sometimes, as in the case of Samuel, one person held all three jobs—chieftain, priest, and prophet.

The greatest challenge facing the tribes was providing military security. Occasional skirmishes were not an issue, for each tribe had its own small army. But defending themselves against an all-out attack by a major foe required a united and powerful army.

Do you find it easier to pray from your heart when you pray silently than when you pray aloud? Why might that be so?

Deborah of Lappidot

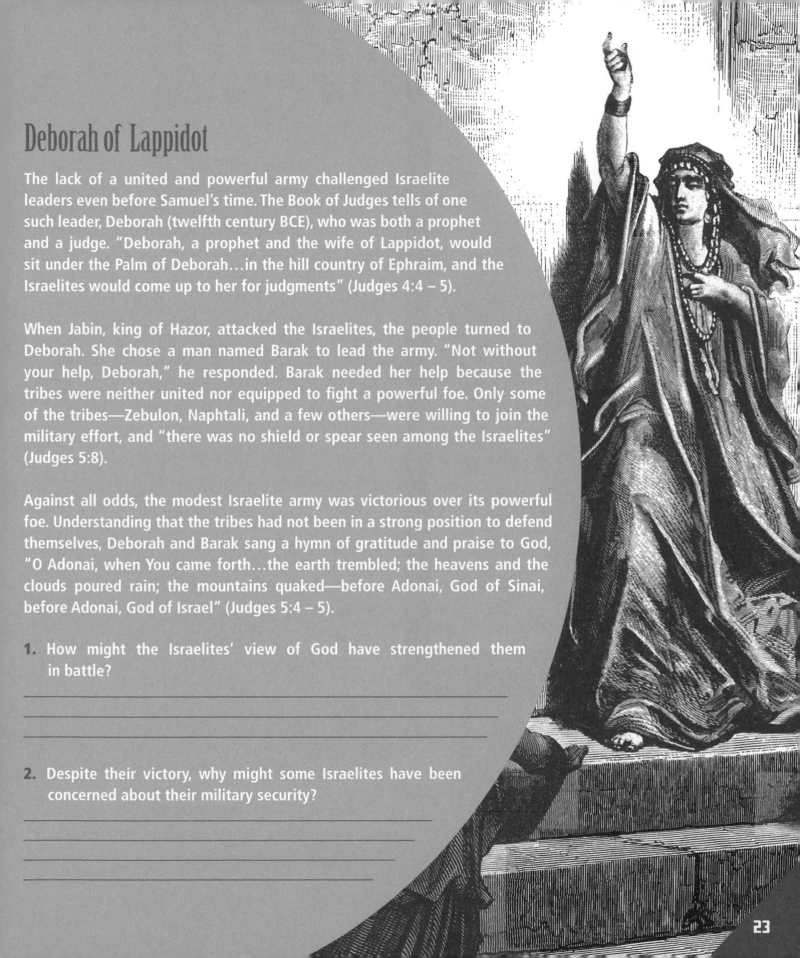

The lack of a united and powerful army challenged Israelite leaders even before Samuel's time. The Book of Judges tells of one such leader, Deborah (twelfth century BCE), who was both a prophet and a judge. "Deborah, a prophet and the wife of Lappidot, would sit under the Palm of Deborah…in the hill country of Ephraim, and the Israelites would come up to her for judgments" (Judges 4:4 – 5).

When Jabin, king of Hazor, attacked the Israelites, the people turned to Deborah. She chose a man named Barak to lead the army. "Not without your help, Deborah," he responded. Barak needed her help because the tribes were neither united nor equipped to fight a powerful foe. Only some of the tribes—Zebulon, Naphtali, and a few others—were willing to join the military effort, and "there was no shield or spear seen among the Israelites" (Judges 5:8).

Against all odds, the modest Israelite army was victorious over its powerful foe. Understanding that the tribes had not been in a strong position to defend themselves, Deborah and Barak sang a hymn of gratitude and praise to God, "O Adonai, when You came forth…the earth trembled; the heavens and the clouds poured rain; the mountains quaked—before Adonai, God of Sinai, before Adonai, God of Israel" (Judges 5:4 – 5).

1. How might the Israelites' view of God have strengthened them in battle?

_____

_____

_____

2. Despite their victory, why might some Israelites have been concerned about their military security?

_____

_____

_____

_____

The Israelite Tribes and Their Neighbors

DAN — Area of Israelite tribes
HIVITES — Non-Israelite people

PHOENICIANS

HIVITES

ARAMEANS

Hazor
CANAANITES
NAPHTALI
ASHER
Mediterranean Sea
Sea of Galilee
ZEBULUN
ISSACHAR

CANAANITES
MANASSEH
Beth-Shean
Shechem
Jordan River

Jaffa
EPHRAIM
Shiloh
GAD
AMMONITES
DAN
BENJAMIN
Ashkelon
Jerusalem
PHILISTINES
CANAANITES
REUBEN
Gaza
Hebron
JUDAH
Dead Sea
SIMEON
MOABITES
EDOMITES
AMALEKITES

N W E S

U.S.
Area of map

0 — 20 MI
0 — 30 KM

The early Israelites were divided into twelve tribes, each with its own portion of land.

Samuel didn't want to create a strong central government, particularly not one headed by a king. True, kings could unite tribal peoples, amass large treasuries, and train powerful armies. But they could also be tyrants. Kings often imposed crushing obligations on their people, including forced labor, military service, and heavy taxes. Added to this was the likelihood that a king would deprive the Israelite tribes of their independence. Samuel hoped that his people, who had heard stories of their ancestors' oppression under Pharaoh, would never agree to such a leader.

Yet, as a deeply religious man, Samuel had an even stronger argument against anointing a king. The model for kingship was Pharaoh and the neighboring god-kings, leaders who were worshipped as earthly forms of the gods. In contrast, Israel's God was the supreme Power, the One and Only Ruler. Furthermore, Israel's God never took on human form. If Samuel were ever to anoint a king, it would be someone who was committed to *serving,* not *being,* God.

Early on, many Israelites shared Samuel's views. But as the tribes spread out across Canaan they realized that their way of life had to change. The looseness of their union—which had protected their independence by keeping all authority local—now threatened their survival. The Israelites needed a strong leader who could unite and arm them against powerful foes. When an enemy arose whose fierceness and lust for power threatened to destroy them, the idea of an earthly king became ever more appealing.

The Tradition of God-Kings

The Egyptians considered their pharaohs gods and called them god-kings. Given the Israelite experience as slaves in Egypt, how do you think our ancestors would have responded to Moses and Samuel if they had represented themselves as god-kings rather than as God's prophets?

_____

_____

What might be the dangers of a leader who believes that he or she is a god, or the dangers of a people who believe, even against their leader's wishes, that their leader is a god?

_____

_____

This painting is from the tomb of Ramses I, one of the pharaohs who ruled during the Israelites' enslavement in ancient Egypt. Ramses reigned from 1292 to 1290 BCE. He is shown standing between Horus, a falcon-headed sky god whose eyes were the sun and the moon, and Anubis, a jackal-headed god of the dead.

What Do You Think?

Many say that monotheism—the belief in one God—is the Jews' greatest gift to civilization. Why might the belief in one God who cares about the well-being of all people be considered so valuable?

_____

_____

TO CHANGE OR NOT TO CHANGE, THAT IS THE QUESTION

Every year, your life changes when you enter a new grade. You may have new teachers, classmates, subjects, and lunch choices, maybe even a new school. To adjust, *you* may need to change. You may need to become more disciplined in doing your homework or less picky about where or what you eat, or take your bike to school instead of the bus. What is new in your school life this year? How have you adapted? How have you stayed the same?

_____

_____

Just like individuals, communities often face situations that require change. In fact, the history of the Jewish people is full of such instances. It began when our ancestors left Egypt and shed their slave mentality to take on the responsibilities of a free people. The need to change continues, even to this day, for new challenges always arise.

In your own words, why did the Israelite tribes need to change to a centralized form of government?

_____

_____

What were their reasons *not* to change?

_____

_____

The Menace of the Philistines

The Philistines were a warrior people. Like many nations in the ancient world, they developed their political and economic power by conquering other peoples. Scholars are uncertain about the origins of the Philistines, but some think they migrated to Canaan from the area around Greece. In time, they developed a foothold on the southern coast of Canaan and then expanded eastward into Israelite territory.

The Philistines outstripped the Israelite warriors in numbers, strength, and unity. In addition, they used what was then an advanced technology—iron weapons and iron-spoke chariots—to charge through enemy lines. Consider how the Israelites must have felt looking out upon the Philistine troops. Had you been an Israelite, how might the scene have affected your desire for a powerful king?

Soon, the Philistines dominated most of Canaan. At Eben-ezer, the Israelites brought the Ark of the Covenant, the symbol of God's power and authority, from Shiloh onto the battlefield. At first, their plan seemed to work. Upon seeing the Ark, "the Philistines were afraid, for they said: 'God has come to the camp….Who will deliver us from the hand of this mighty God, Elohim, who struck the Egyptians with every kind of plague in the wilderness?'" (1 Samuel 4:7 – 8).

But despite the Israelites' best hopes and the Philistines' worst fears, the Philistines triumphed.

Imagine how the Philistines must have swaggered! They had slaughtered thousands of their foes and captured the Ark of the Covenant. The surviving Israelites fled, convinced that God's glory had departed with their Ark.

The Book of Samuel describes the Philistines' return to their city of Ashdod. They carried the Ark triumphantly into the temple of Dagon, their chief god, and set it as a tribute next to the sculpture of Dagon—a figure with the head and hands of a human and the body of a fish. But early next morning, to the horror of Ashdod's citizens, Dagon's statue lay face down, humbled before the Ark. The Philistines quickly set the statue upright in its place, but the following day it lay shattered on the ground with its head and hands cut off.

Tradition teaches that the shattering of Dagon was only the first sign of God's wrath against the Philistines. Soon, the city of Ashdod descended into the agonies of a plague. Each time the Philistines relocated the Ark, the plague followed. After seven months, the terrified victors returned the Ark to the Israelites.

Samuel Defeats the Philistines

Although the Ark was now in Israelite hands, it had been desecrated. Furthermore, the Philistines continued to oppress Israel. The Israelites must have thought that Adonai had deserted them or, worse yet, that God was weak. Humiliated and demoralized, they abandoned their worship of Adonai and served their conquerors' gods.

How might Samuel have felt seeing his people lose their faith and worship foreign gods?

In the aftermath of the Israelites' defeat, how difficult might it have been to stand up and speak of a more powerful force than the Philistines?

How might you have responded as a prophet?

These weapons are from the period when the Philistines were developing a foothold in the Israelites' territory. The dagger handle is bronze and the blade is iron. Iron was harder and more durable than earlier metals that were used for blades.

The Ark of the Covenant

The Ark of the Covenant was a chest made of acacia wood and covered—inside and out—in pure gold. According to tradition, the Ark housed the stone tablets of the Ten Commandments.

Samuel had complete faith in God. He had no doubts even when the Philistines triumphed and seized the Ark. But the Israelites did not share his steadfast loyalty.

Alone in his faith, Samuel approached Adonai as his mother had. Speaking silently in his heart, he prayed that Israel's faith would be reborn.

Finally, twenty years after the Philistines had brought back the Ark, a yearning for Adonai returned throughout Israel. When Samuel walked among the people they no longer turned away. Instead they sought him out. Like their ancestors in Egypt, they now were eager to break the bonds of oppression.

"If you return to Adonai with all your heart, remove the foreign gods, and serve only Adonai," Samuel said to the Israelites, "God will forgive you and deliver you from the stranglehold of the Philistines."

The people heeded Samuel's words. They removed the foreign gods and served only Adonai.

—inspired by 1 Samuel 7:2 – 4

Twenty years later, when the Philistines attacked again, the Israelites triumphed. Tradition teaches that "the hand of Adonai was against the Philistines all the days of Samuel…. And Samuel judged Israel all the days of his life" (1 Samuel 7:13, 15).

"Give Us a King"

Years passed and Samuel became an elderly man. Concerned that he had no worthy successor and that the Philistines would once again triumph over them, the Israelites stood before Samuel and said, "Give us a king to govern us" (1 Samuel 8:6). Reluctant to do so, Samuel warned:

> This will be the way of the king who will rule over you. He will take your sons and make them his charioteers and horsemen, and they will run before his chariot….they will have to plow his fields, reap his harvest, and make his weapons….He will turn your daughters into perfumers, cooks, and bakers. He will seize your best fields, vineyards, and olive groves, and give them to his servants….you shall become his slaves.
> —1 Samuel 8:11 – 17

Samuel was right. That was the way of earthly kings up until that time. But the truth behind the people's plea could not be ignored: Only a united Israel could defeat the enemies it faced. A new era in Israel's history was about to begin.

The Shephelah, or Judean foothills, is in south-central Israel. In Samuel's time, the Shephelah was the main battleground between the Israelites and the Philistines. In modern times, its fertile soil and natural springs have led to its agricultural development.

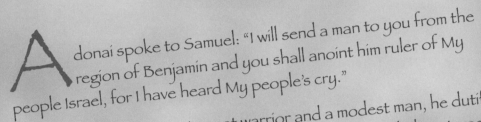

Adonai spoke to Samuel: "I will send a man to you from the region of Benjamin and you shall anoint him ruler of My people Israel, for I have heard My people's cry."

Saul was God's chosen. A great warrior and a modest man, he dutifully came to Samuel in the city of Ramah. Although Samuel's heart was heavy, he set aside his doubts about anointing a king and went to the open countryside with Saul. There the prophet took a flask of oil and anointed Saul, saying, "Adonai now crowns you ruler over the people of Israel."

With those words, the spirit of God entered Saul, that he might serve God and honor the Covenant as Israel's king.

—based on 1 Samuel 9:15 – 16, 10:1, 10:6

"When Samuel saw Saul, Adonai declared, 'this is the man whom I told you would reign over my people'" (1 Samuel 9:17).

The Conscience of the King and the People

To limit the power of the king, checks and balances were put in place. The king was the civil ruler and army commander-in-chief; the priests and the prophets were the religious leaders. The priests conducted the sacrificial rites at an official altar, and the prophets instructed the people and the king in God's law.

In other nations, the king's word was law and could not be questioned. Among the Israelites, there was a higher law, God's law, and people were taught to question laws made by humans. Other nations worshipped their kings. The Israelites were taught never to idolize another human—not kings, not the rich, not the famous, not the beautiful, not even the prophets.

We can thank Samuel for that. He understood that the people would have their king with or without his blessing. So he established the kingship on the principle of service to God, to justice, and to mercy. He taught that, like everyone else, Israelite kings were responsible for upholding the ethics and values of the Covenant.

Some kings honored that principle more than others. But always there were prophets to remind them and their subjects of why they had been liberated from Egypt and to inspire them to live as a holy people.

Historical Note

The Kingdom Unites then Cracks

It turned out that Saul was not a strong leader. In fact, the chapters of the Bible that tell of his reign describe him more like a chieftain than a king. The territory he controlled was not very large, and he had no palace or capital city. Although he was a great warrior, Saul was unable to unite the Israelites. It was Israel's second king, David, who succeeded in uniting them.

David crushed the Philistines once and for all so that they no longer posed a threat to Israel's survival. He also captured the city of Jerusalem, establishing it as the kingdom's political and religious capital. During the more than thirty years of his reign, King David unified the bitterly divided people and developed Israel into one of the strongest powers in the region.

In about 967 BCE King David appointed his son Solomon as heir to the throne. Solomon developed Israel into a center of international trade but is best remembered for building the Temple in Jerusalem. Despite his accomplishments, King Solomon's reign created religious conflicts and economic problems that weakened the kingdom. He heavily taxed the population and required forced labor for his building projects.

When Solomon died in 928 BCE, his kingdom cracked in two: Israel in the north and Judah in the south. In place of the strong, united kingdom there were now two small, weak states that were often hostile to one another and vulnerable to attack by their neighbors.

Let's Make a Midrash

Write a short midrash or create a drawing that portrays
Samuel as he struggles with the idea of anointing an earthly
king. Before you begin, imagine that you are in his position.
What might you be thinking and feeling as you struggle to
adjust your views and find a practical solution?

_____

_____

_____

_____

_____

_____

_____

_____

_____

_____

_____

_____

In the Footsteps of the Prophets

Yitzḥak Rabin

Like many ancient Israelite judges and prophets, Yitzḥak Rabin (1922 – 1995) was a military and government leader. Specifically, Rabin was a senior military commander and then became prime minister of the modern State of Israel. During his first term as prime minister (1974–1977) he ordered a daring raid on the airport in Entebbe, Uganda, after terrorists hijacked an Air France jetliner there. The raid freed all but three of the 105 Jewish hostages.

Standing with their Nobel Peace Prize, from left to right: Yasir Arafat, Shimon Peres, and Yitzḥak Rabin.

In Rabin's second term as prime minister (1992–1995), his goals shifted from winning wars to winning peace. In 1994, Rabin, Shimon Peres (a former Israeli prime minister), and the Palestinian leader Yasir Arafat jointly were awarded the Nobel Peace Prize for their efforts to bring peace to the Middle East.

After negotiating the peace agreement with Arafat in 1993, Rabin said, "I would have liked to sign a peace agreement with Holland, or Luxembourg, or New Zealand. But there was no need to…. One does not make peace with one's friends. One makes peace with one's enemies.

What do you think Rabin meant?

_____

_____

How might you apply his idea to your own life?

_____

_____

In what ways was Rabin like the prophets you've studied?

_____

_____

Go To http://www.TheJewishProphets.com ▼

CHAPTER ④ Elijah:
Zealous Critic of the King

Day Six: By mid-afternoon the world was teeming with majestic creations of every sort: sunlight that spilled over the seas and dry land, and a glorious array of plants, fish, birds, insects, and wild beasts. Now God was ready to create the crowning glory—human beings.

As the new creature took form, Sandalphon leaned forward for a better view. Imagining future generations, the angel thought, "I shall weave Israel's prayers into garlands. Yet surely there is more that I can do." Unable to contain himself, Sandalphon cried out, "Master of the universe! If it pleases You, I will descend to earth to make myself of service to humans."

God smiled. Some angels had argued against the creation of humankind. They had no faith in its goodness. But Sandalphon would show that with a little help humans could tend to the world, even improve it. "Yes, Sandalphon's idea is good," thought God, "very good, indeed."

Before sending the angel to live among the humans, God gave him the earthly name Elijah and instructed him, "Be the guardian spirit of My children forever, and spread belief in Me throughout the world."

As he accepted his mission, a fiery chariot with fiery horses appeared, and Elijah was swept in a whirlwind down to earth.

—based on Genesis 1; 2 Kings 2:11; Talmud, Sanhedrin 38a; Pardes Rimmonim; Emek Hamelech, Zohar vol. 2, 58a

PROPHET'S PROFILE: ELIJAH

BEGINNINGS:

- Born in the ninth century BCE, Elijah was from Gilead, a mountainous region in the northern kingdom of Israel.
- Hebrew Name: Eliyahu, meaning "my God is Adonai."
- Archenemies: King Ahab and Queen Jezebel of Israel.

PERSONAL:

- Famous Guest Appearance: Elijah appears as a vagrant in Herman Melville's 1851 novel *Moby-Dick*. He reprimands the characters Ishmael and Queequeg for sailing with Ahab, the tyrannical and cruel captain of the whaling ship Pequod.

POSTS:

Who was Elijah?

Biblical Buzz: The prophet Malachi says that Elijah will reappear on earth as a sign of the coming of the Messiah, and he will make peace between "parents and their children and between children and their parents…" (Malachi 3:23 – 24).

Favorite Song: "Eliyahu Hanavi."

Preferred Mode of Travel: Fiery chariots with fiery horses fueled by whirlwinds.

Favorite Quotation: In response to Ahab's bullying, the prophet said: "I did not bring trouble on Israel; it was caused by your abandonment of Adonai's *mitzvot* and your pursuit of foreign gods" (I Kings 18:18).

Major Contribution: Serving as the conscience of Israel, Elijah kept the king in check. He was an example to future prophets who would also speak boldly against the people's behavior.

Go To | http://www.TheJewishProphets.com

The Man and the Mystery

The story of Elijah is veiled in mystery. When we first meet him in the Bible's 1 Kings, he appears without fanfare or introduction—as if out of the blue—to confront King Ahab, ruler of the northern kingdom of Israel. His story ends in 2 Kings in a dramatic passage that describes how, after passing his authority on to the prophet Elisha, a fiery chariot with fiery horses sweeps him up to heaven in a whirlwind.

The Bible tells us nothing of Elijah's birth or death, or even *if* he died. In fact, it tells us precious little about who the prophet was and what he did, devoting only six of the forty-seven chapters in the Book of Kings to him. Yet the power of what the Bible *does* say about Elijah—especially his passionate loyalty to God and to the people of Israel—is so great that it has inspired countless legends and folktales that glorify his name.

Will the Real Elijah Please Stand Up?

Jewish tradition has created a rich and complex portrait of Elijah by drawing on diverse sources—the Bible, legend, and folklore. Each source provides a unique view of the prophet plus down-to-earth life lessons spiced with miraculous events. The Bible, for example, portrays Elijah as a stern prophet quick to reprimand those who err, while rabbinic legend and folklore often describe him as a more kindly, even playful, character who is dedicated to helping those in need.

So, who is the real Elijah? Is he stern or kindly, quick to reprimand or quick to offer a helping hand? Is he all those things or none of them? Is he one character or several different people?

Perhaps instead of deciding we should figure out what we can learn from our tradition's stories. Just as we tell the tale of George Washington and the cherry tree knowing that the truth is not in the story but rather in its moral—honesty is important—so, too, we value the Jewish tradition of storytelling for the richness of its teachings, even when the "facts" of the story are unclear.

All the stories of Elijah can enrich our understanding of Jewish beliefs and values. They live on because they inspire our hope for a better world and teach us how to turn our hope into reality.

What Color Is the Real You?

Like the portrait of Elijah, a portrait of any human being is complex because each person has many different aspects. No one is always happy or sad, strong or weak, confident or fearful.

Imagine that different traits and feelings are colors on an artist's palette. Then complete the statements below to determine some of the colors for your self-portrait.

1. When I'm happy, color me _____

2. When I'm grouchy, color me _____

3. When I'm sad, color me _____

4. When I'm kind, color me _____

5. When I'm helpful, color me _____

6. When I'm _____ , color me _____

As you read this chapter, think about what Elijah can teach about faith, commitment, and courage, and what you might want to ask him about how to handle fear or self-doubt. Think about who in today's world or in your personal life reminds you of the prophet and why.

What about your personality or character would you most want a portrait of yourself to reveal to others? Why?

PHOENICIANS

Dan

DAMASCUS

Sea of Galilee

Mediterranean Sea

ISRAEL (Northern Kingdom)

ARAM

Samaria

—Jordan River

Beth-el Jericho

Jerusalem

AMMON

Gaza

Hebron

Dead Sea

PHILISTIA

Beer-sheba

MOAB

EDOM

JUDAH (Southern Kingdom)

N
W — E
S

Ezion Geber

U.S.

Area of map

0   20 MI
0   30 KM

Red Sea

After the death of King Solomon, the kingdom was divided in two: Israel in the north and Judah in the south.

The Wicked King and the "Troublemaker of Israel"

It was a desperate time. A three-year drought had parched the fields of Israel, turning its crops to dust. Elijah had warned Ahab in God's name, "There will be no dew or rain unless I call it forth" (1 Kings 17:1). But the wicked king turned away from God and served Baal—the god of his foreign, non-Israelite wife Jezebel. He even built a temple for Baal in Samaria, Israel's capital.

Determined to spread Jezebel's religion throughout the land, the king publicly worshipped Baal as lord of the rain. All went according to plan. Following their king's example, most of the people worshipped Baal, too. When groups of Israelite prophets wandered the kingdom pleading with the Israelites to remain faithful to God, the ruthless Jezebel had them slaughtered.

An enraged Elijah met with Ahab, who accused him of being a "troublemaker." Undeterred, Elijah demanded that Ahab gather the 450 prophets of Baal and the 400 prophets of the goddess Asherah at Mount Carmel in the presence of the entire nation of Israel. The king summoned the public, probably hoping to discredit Elijah once and for all.

The prophet slowly rose to his feet, a tall, lean figure dressed in a loincloth and a hairy robe. Never before had he so publicly put his beliefs on the line. He could feel the tension rising in his neck. His long, gray hair and thick beard were practically standing on end. Fixing his eyes on the throng of Israelites, Elijah cried out, "How long will you hop between two beliefs? If Adonai be God, follow Adonai; but if Baal, then follow him."

Hearing no response, Elijah continued, "Bring two young bulls and let the prophets of Baal choose one, cut it up, and lay it on the wood for sacrifice without placing a fire under it. I will prepare the second bull in the same way."

The sole prophet of God now turned to his horde of competitors shouting, "Call to your god by name and I will call to Adonai. Let us agree: the god who responds with fire is the true God."

The contest was now officially underway. The prophets of Baal quickly readied their bull and built their altar. Then they confidently called to Baal. But there was no response. So they danced around the altar, shouting louder and louder. But still there was no answer.

Elijah called the Israelites closer to him as he readied the other bull. He built a large trench around the altar and asked that water be poured over the altar so that it overflowed into the trench. When all was done, the prophet called out to God, "Answer me, O Adonai. Answer me." A fire immediately came down. It consumed the bull, the wood, the altar, and the earth around it until it licked up the water from the trench.

Humbled, the Israelites fell to the ground on their faces, crying out, "Adonai alone is God! Adonai Hu ha'Elohim!"

—based on 1 Kings 18:21 – 39

Yom Kippur Declaration

At the end of Yom Kippur, as the sun is about to set, we make the same declaration as did our ancestors on Mount Carmel: Adonai alone is God! *Adonai Hu ha'Elohim* (1 Kings: 18:39). As a community we announce, as our ancestors did, that there is but one God.

Do you think this is a fitting way to end our holiday prayers? Why? What false gods, such as money, beauty, popularity, and fame, are worshipped today? What problems can worshipping them create?

Soon after the gathering at Mount Carmel, the sound of thunder rumbled across the sky. A cloud arose from the sea and a great rain came over Israel. The drought was over.

A Still, Small Voice

Jezebel wanted Elijah dead. She'd heard about the scene on Mount Carmel, and she learned that every last prophet of Baal who had been present had been slaughtered at Wadi Kishon.

Fearing for his life, Elijah fled to the wilderness until he came to Mount Horeb, the same mountain on which Moses had encountered the burning bush. Elijah went into a cave and spent the night there. God came to Elijah, calling him to come out of the cave's darkness.

> …Behold Adonai passed by. There was a great and powerful wind, splitting mountains and shattering rocks by the might of Adonai. But Adonai was not in the wind. After the wind came an earthquake. But Adonai was not in the earthquake. After the earthquake came a fire. But Adonai was not in the fire. And after the fire, there came a still, small voice.
>
> When Elijah heard it, he wrapped his robe over his face and went out and stood at the entrance to the cave. Then a voice spoke to him: "Why are you here, Elijah?"
>
> —1 Kings 19:11 – 13

As complex as human portraits may be, the Bible portrays God in an even more complicated way. Rich with variations and contradictions, God is sometimes portrayed as loving and kind; sometimes as angry and vengeful. Sometimes God's voice is described as loud and bold as thunder, and sometimes as soft and gentle as a murmur.

The clatter of our emotions and busy schedules can make it difficult for us to hear the voice of godliness when it is soft. For example, the ring of a phone or blare of traffic may drown out the quiet voice of our conscience.

So here's a tip: Not only can Jewish rituals, such as celebrating Shabbat and reciting daily blessings, help calm us by providing a peaceful island in time, they can also be like "spiritual amps" that raise the volume of the godly voice to help refresh and strengthen our souls. *Why might such rituals simultaneously calm us and amplify the voice of godliness?*

It's Not Just Unfair—It's Murder!

By the time Elijah left Mount Horeb, he was ready to resume his mission. It was a good thing, too, because Ahab and Jezebel were up to no good.

The ritual blowing of the shofar, or ram's horn, at Rosh Hashanah prayer services and at the end of Yom Kippur is like a godly wake-up call. It reminds us that while no one is perfect, each of us can work to do our best.

WHERE IS GOD?

A Hasidic rabbi was once asked where God could be found. He answered, "Wherever people let God in." How might this explain why Elijah found God in a cave in the wilderness?

_____

_____

If you can, describe a time when you felt God in your life.

_____

_____

If you can, describe a time when you wanted or expected to feel God in your life but didn't.

_____

_____

Describe one way people can let God into their lives by being just or merciful.

_____

_____

Nabot wouldn't budge. The vineyard had been in his family for as long as he could remember, and he wasn't giving it up. Not even for the king. But Ahab wanted it. Badly. It sat conveniently near the palace grounds, begging to become a royal vegetable garden. Or so the king thought.

Nabot didn't care. He stood firm, even when the king offered him the generous choice of a better vineyard or a princely sum. So Ahab returned to the palace, lay down on his bed, and refused to eat. When Jezebel heard what had dispirited her royal spouse, she said, "Now is the time to show everyone who is king over Israel. You eat and I'll get the vineyard for you."

Jezebel got right down to work. She had Nabot framed for a crime and arranged for two false witnesses to testify against him. The innocent vintner was quickly condemned then stoned to death, leaving Ahab free to claim the vineyard as his trophy.

Hearing what had happened, Elijah confronted the king. "Would you murder and take possession, passing yourself off as an heir?" Continuing in God's name, Elijah warned: "In the very place where the dogs lapped up Nabot's blood, the dogs will lap up your blood and devour Jezebel, too."

—based on 1 Kings 21:1 – 23

How did Elijah find the courage to deliver such terrifying news? God's laws must have rung in his ears as they did on Mount Sinai: Do not murder. Do not steal. Do not bear false witness. Do not desire what belongs to your neighbor. The prophet's religious beliefs surely guided and emboldened him. Justice must be pursued. Even the king must be held accountable.

FOLLOW ME

Kings and politicians aren't the only leaders. A prophet also must be willing to lead. Below are ten traits of a good leader. Put checks next to the three that best describe Elijah. Put stars next to the three that best describe you.

___ Strong communicator   ___ Trustworthy and honest

___ Good listener   ___ Open-minded

___ Self-confident   ___ Responsible and reliable

___ Person of courage   ___ Inspiring

___ Good decision maker   ___ Flexible

___ Other: _____

If you could suggest to Elijah that he develop or strengthen one trait that you did not check off for him, what would it be? Which additional trait might you want to develop or strengthen in yourself?
What step could you take to accomplish your goal?

_____

_____

It is often said that great leaders are made not born. What do you think that means? Do you agree or disagree? If you could teach a child one important lesson to help him or her become a strong leader, what would that be?

Most of us have several authority figures in our lives—parents, grandparents, teachers, principals, rabbis, and coaches, to name but a few. Generally, such people are helpful and supportive, even fun. But sometimes we may disagree with them and want to speak up. Why might it be more challenging to speak up to an authority figure than to a friend? How might you address the challenge?

Tradition teaches that Elijah appears from time to time disguised as a stranger to help us when we are in trouble. It is also said that he will come to announce the Messiah, the time when peace will reign throughout the world. At the Passover seder, we welcome Elijah with hope and faith by filling a large cup with wine and opening our door to him.

A Meddler or a Mensch?

Was Elijah a meddler who couldn't keep his nose out of royal affairs or a mensch—a decent person—who couldn't walk away from injustice? What made him so zealous, so passionate about setting things right? *What gave him the courage and determination to speak up?*

Elijah challenged the corrupt leadership of his day because he believed in God's teachings and that members of the Covenant are obligated to pursue justice, even when it puts them at risk. He spoke up when others didn't because he thought that it was far more dangerous to be silent and risk evil taking over than it was to confront evil. He took action because he was not prepared to let the bullies win.

When we study the Bible, we hear Elijah's godly message to pay attention to the world around us. He teaches us to notice when people suffer and when leaders stray from sacred values, such as honesty and trustworthiness. He asks, "Are you willing to leave the comfort of your daily life and work for change? *How can you work with others to pursue justice?"*

The prophet's questions call out to us, no matter our age or our circumstance. We each can make a difference—in our homes, our classrooms, our sports teams, and our synagogues. Jewish traditions and rituals can provide the spiritual amps that strengthen our souls and give us courage. Guided by the still, small voice within us, we can speak up as honestly as we know how and join others who share our concerns.

It's true. Together, we not only can care for the world, we can also improve it and make some friends along the way.

Bella Abzug

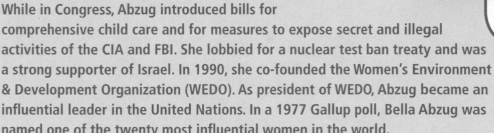

Bella Abzug

Bella Abzug (1920 – 1998) was born in the Bronx, in New York City. As a young girl, she played marbles and checkers, traded baseball cards, attended religious school, and joined Hashomer Hatzair, a Zionist youth movement. When she grew up, she became a lawyer dedicated to defending women's rights and speaking out against racism, prejudice, and the violence of war. In 1970, she became the first Jewish woman to serve in the U.S. Congress.

While in Congress, Abzug introduced bills for comprehensive child care and for measures to expose secret and illegal activities of the CIA and FBI. She lobbied for a nuclear test ban treaty and was a strong supporter of Israel. In 1990, she co-founded the Women's Environment & Development Organization (WEDO). As president of WEDO, Abzug became an influential leader in the United Nations. In a 1977 Gallup poll, Bella Abzug was named one of the twenty most influential women in the world.

Like Elijah, Abzug was known for her striking appearance, particularly her large and flamboyant hats. And like Elijah, she was not afraid to speak her mind. She once played off a West African proverb that Theodore Roosevelt liked to quote, "Speak softly but carry a big stick; you will go far," saying, "Women have been trained to speak softly and carry a lipstick. Those days are over."

What do you think Abzug meant?

_____

_____

How might Abzug's religious education and commitment have helped her speak up?

_____

_____

Go To http://www.TheJewishProphets.com ▼

45

CHAPTER 5 Amos:
Faithful Friend of the Covenant

Amos climbed the rugged hills of Judah in silence, his herd of nokdim—small speckled sheep—following closely behind. Like their shepherd, they were a hardy and exceptional breed. The nokdim thrived in the harsh desert climate with little food and water, yet their wool was thick and luxurious.

Surveying the horizon, Amos looked for relief from the noonday sun. He soon spied a lone sycamore with sprawling branches the breadth of several ordinary trees. Pleased, he led his flock toward its shade. But the sheep stopped short of the tree and would not budge. As Amos began to prod them he heard God speak from deep within the sycamore.

The Voice was loud and insistent, like the roar of a lion: "Amos, go prophesy to My people Israel for they have strayed far from Me, pursuing gods of corruption and greed."

A quiet and shy soul, Amos could not imagine speaking before a crowd. "I am not a prophet, nor the son of a prophet," Amos protested. "I am a sheep breeder and farmer—a caretaker of sycamore figs."

But God had spoken and Amos had heard, so he went north to prophesy in Israel.

—inspired by Amos 3:7 – 8, 7:14 – 15

PROPHET'S PROFILE: AMOS

BEGINNINGS:

- Born in the early eighth century BCE in Tekoa, on the edge of the Judean wilderness, twelve miles south of Jerusalem, the capital of Judah.
- Hebrew Name: Amos, meaning "burdened."

PERSONAL:

- Began to prophesy in about 750 BCE, toward the end of the reigns of Uzziah, king of Judah, and Jeroboam II, king of Israel.
- Prophesied in the kingdom of Israel, mostly in Bethel, an important religious center, and in Samaria, the kingdom's capital.

POSTS:

Who was Amos?

Favorite Quotation: "Let justice flow like water, righteousness like a mighty stream" (Amos 5:24).

Favorite Pastime: Tending sheep and fig trees.

Biggest Fear: Public speaking.

Greatest Loss When He Left Judah: The peace and quiet of country life.

Major Contribution: Taught that social justice, or concern for the people who have the greatest needs, is at the heart of all good societies and key to the survival of the Jewish people.

Go To http://www.TheJewishProphets.com ▼

47

Who Can Ignore the Roar of the Lion?

We know almost nothing about Amos's personal life except that he came from the village of Tekoa. No records exist of his mom, dad, or siblings. We don't know if he had a wife or children, friends or foes. But the little we do know suggests that Amos lived a humble rather than a privileged life and that he probably felt more comfortable tending his flock and the sycamore trees than speaking in public.

So why would a modest man accustomed to a quiet, rural life agree to leave his home and all that was dear to him to confront a group of affluent city folk whom he didn't know? Why was he willing to question the behavior of strangers and risk their rejection or, worse yet, their ridicule and anger?

The Bible teaches that, having heard God's call as the roar of a lion, Amos felt he had no choice but to speak up for what was right.

Have you ever heard the voice of goodness or justice—you may sometimes call it your conscience—deep inside you?

Unlike Moses, who was raised in a palace, and Samuel, who was raised in Jerusalem's Temple, Amos probably had little or no experience dealing with socially and politically powerful people. Do you think that made him less or more qualified to be a prophet than Moses and Samuel? Why? Amos's name means "burdened." Do you think he felt his mission was a burden or an opportunity?

Maybe you heard it after seeing someone being bullied or teased or after a teacher made a rule that you thought was unfair. Why did you want to speak up or take action after hearing the voice? *Has the discomfort of standing out from the crowd ever made you think twice about speaking up? What has or could help you overcome such concerns?*

Amos Prophesies at the Temple in Bethel

Imagine how Amos, a humble shepherd, might have felt when he arrived in the kingdom of Israel and walked the affluent streets of Bethel.

Had you been at his side, what might you have thought or felt? How might you have encouraged him?

The wealthy citizens of Bethel arose from their ivory beds, bowed before their idols, drank their fill of wine, then tipsily made their way, dressed in fine wool and linen, along the city streets. Several children smirked as they passed Amos, who wore a shepherd's simple robe.

The prophet hardly noticed their contempt as he quickly walked to the temple. Arriving at its outer courtyard, he stood before a small crowd and began to prophesy God's wrath against the six nations who surrounded the kingdom of Israel—Damascus (Syria), Gaza (Philistia), Tyre (Phoenicia), Edom, Ammon, and Moab.

One after the other, Amos named their sins: the cruelty of kings, the heartless enslavement of captives, the pitiless violence against neighboring states, the extreme violence against women and children, and the dishonoring of the dead. He also named God's punishment: the destruction of all six kingdoms.

Each time the prophet introduced a kingdom he began with these words, "Thus said Adonai: For the three sins of the following kingdom, I might have offered forgiveness, but because of the fourth, I will not take back My punishment."

By now, Amos's audience was an overflowing crowd. Its members were Bethel's wealthiest citizens, for the poor no longer could afford the price of temple sacrifices. Enthusiastically hooting and jeering, the rowdy horde delighted in God's condemnation of the neighboring kingdoms. Secure in their belief that as members of the Covenant Judah and Israel were God's chosen, they felt protected from misfortune.

Then Amos proclaimed, "Thus said Adonai: For the three sins of Judah, I might have offered forgiveness. but because of the fourth, I will not take back My punishment."

The crowd froze. If Judah was threatened, then Israel, too, might no longer be safe.

—based on Amos 1:1 – 2:4

After prophesying Judah's destruction, its punishment for not honoring God's laws, Amos tells the citizens of Israel what they already had begun to fear:

Thus said Adonai:
For the three sins of Israel,
I might have offered forgiveness,
But because of the fourth,
I will not take back My punishment.
For they betray the righteous for silver
And the needy for a pair of sandals.
You…trample the heads of the poor
Into the dust of the earth…
And order the prophets not to preach.

—Amos 2:4 – 7, 12

Imagine how these declarations must have shocked Amos's audience. They had been so sure that as God's beloved, Judah and Israel would be immune to punishment. Had God forgotten their partnership, the Covenant? Had Amos?

No. Ironically, it was the Jewish people who had forgotten.

As in biblical times, sheep and goats are herded in Israel today. But digital technologies, such as computers and cell phones, have decreased the gap between rural and urban Israelis. Had such technologies existed in ancient times, would you have advised Amos to use them to prophesy from home rather than show up in person, or would you have suggest that he do both? Why?

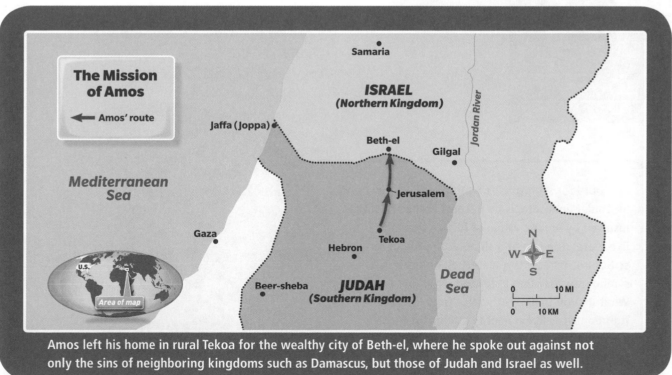

Amos left his home in rural Tekoa for the wealthy city of Beth-el, where he spoke out against not only the sins of neighboring kingdoms such as Damascus, but those of Judah and Israel as well.

After confronting the people with their wrongdoing and urging them to repent by honoring the Covenant, Amos prayed, "O God, Adonai, forgive [the people of Israel]" (Amos 7:2).

Why do you think Amos prayed for the people's forgiveness rather than for severe punishment?

_____

_____

Do you think Amos's prayer was a sign of his strength or his weakness?

_____

_____

The Call to Honor the Covenant

If our ancestors had imagined that the Covenant gave them a special status that put them above God's just and compassionate laws, Amos was there to proclaim that they were wrong. The humble peasant from Tekoa confronted the Israelites with their shameless disregard of ethical responsibility. On behalf of God, Amos asked our ancestors to repent by living righteous lives.

> You alone have I chosen
> from all the families of the earth.
> That is why I will hold you responsible
> for all your wrongdoing….
> Seek Adonai, and you shall live,
> Or God will consume the House of Joseph
> [the northern kingdom] with fire,
> And there will be no one in Bethel
> to put out the flames….
> Establish justice at the gates of the city,
> Then perhaps God will be compassionate to the
> survivors of Joseph….
> Let justice flow like water, righteousness
> like a mighty stream."
> —Amos 3:2, 5:6, 5:15, 5:24

This outdoor sculpture at Temple of Aaron in St. Paul, Minnesota, is by Herbert Ferber. It was inspired by Amos's vision of justice flowing like water. The rotating circle at the top of the sculpture represents a waterfall; below it is a symbol representing a flowing stream of water. What do you think "Let justice flow like water, righteousness like a mighty stream" means? What other quotation from Amos could you express as a piece of art? How?

The Times They Are A-Changin'

In 1963, Bob Dylan, a Jewish songwriter and singer, wrote "The Times They Are A-Changin'." The 1960s was a decade of social unrest—most particularly, it gave birth to the civil rights movement and the protest against the war in Vietnam. It was a time when hundreds of people were jailed or killed as they worked to create a more just world. Dylan's lyrics warned people that society was changing and that they would be left behind if they didn't change. He says "Come writers and critics who prophesize with your pen, and keep your eyes wide, the chance won't come again."

Bob Dylan playing harmonica and guitar, in about 1965.

What do you think the lyrics mean?

_____
_____
_____

How might a writer prophesy and inspire with a song, a story, or a blog?

_____
_____
_____

Is it important for prophets to continue to speak up even if people don't take action on their words? Why or why not?

_____
_____
_____

What Became of the People Israel?

According to the Book of Kings, more than twenty–thousand Israelites were deported to Babylonia (the birthplace of Abraham) and to Elam, in the interior of the Assyrian empire. They eventually became known as "the ten lost tribes."

The Price of Corruption and Greed

Despite Amos's best efforts, the people of Israel did not repent, and their kingdom was destroyed in 722 BCE by the Assyrians (a powerful empire in the area that is now Iraq).

Why might a society that mistreats many of its citizens, including orphans and the poor, become weak?

How can corruption and greed increase a nation's vulnerability to attack from internal or external forces?

Think about today's world. How might a nation put itself at risk by depriving millions of its citizens of adequate food, housing, and medical attention? What might be the consequences to a community if thousands of its children

DO THE RIGHT THING

Amos, who is sometimes called the prophet of social justice, reminds us that as members of the Covenant we are required to uphold God's just laws. For example, we are obligated to help feed and clothe the poor, and help free the oppressed. But it isn't always clear when or how to respond to injustice—such as an unfair school dress code or a human rights violation.

When you don't know what, if anything, to do, you might ask yourself these questions:

1. What is wrong?

2. What words or actions could turn the wrong into a right, or improve the situation?

3. What, if anything, do I want to say or do?

Imagine that you received a link to a video on YouTube that mocked a classmate. How might you answer the three questions?

1. _____

2. _____

3. _____

If you were to encounter a situation in which you were not able to answer the three questions to your satisfaction, to whom would you go for help? Why?

_____

_____

are denied a quality education and therefore lack the skills to become firefighters, teachers, scientists, and architects? How might a family or circle of friends be weakened if some members only *accept* rather than *offer* kindness and love?

These many centuries after the fall of the kingdom of Israel Amos still inspires and teaches us through his words. He asks us—as he asked our ancestors—to uphold the Covenant by pursuing the godly values of justice and peace. When we learn of people who go to bed hungry or who are oppressed by violence in far-off lands or in our own country or community, it is Amos who proclaims that we must take action.

He reminds us of our duty to contribute tzedakah, write to a politician, or join a demonstration on behalf of those who suffer. Amos also asks us to question how we treat our classmates, especially those whom we may not like so much. And it is Amos who jogs our memory when we become self-centered. He speaks directly to our conscience, teaching us to help our parents when they are tired or ill or out-of-sorts and need kindness, concern, and forgiveness.

Amos overcame his shyness, left his comfort zone, and stood up for what he believed, in hopes of inspiring the kingdom of Israel to honor the Covenant. Although our ancestors did not heed his words, through his prophesies Amos continues to urge our people to remember the Jewish commitment to justice and to keep the hope of a better world alive. We hear his message when we study his writings and when we make efforts to step beyond the limits of our comfort zone.

Who knows what will be a lifesaver to the next person? Sometimes we may think that a small act of kindness, like running an errand for a busy parent or tutoring a friend in math, isn't important. But such small acts often provide people with the support they need to keep afloat.

Must I Stand Up Alone?

Amos's belief that his cause was just and that God had chosen him as a prophet gave him the confidence and determination to speak out against wrongdoing. But standing up for what you believe is right doesn't require that you "fly solo." Often it is helpful to join others who share your concerns; for example, find a social action group that helps those in need, or seek out friends, teachers, or family members with whom you can discuss the issues.

What advice would you give a friend who said that he or she doesn't feel comfortable speaking out in a group?

_____

_____

Poll Your Friends: With all the social networking available through the internet, it is easier and easier to find others who share your concerns and interests. Try this: think of a cause you care about—humane treatment of animals, for example. See how many groups you can find on your favorite networking sites that work for this same cause. Then use your phone or your computer to poll your friends—how many can you find who feel the same way you do?

Ruth Bader Ginsburg

Ruth Bader Ginsburg (b. 1933) was sworn in as the 107th justice to the U.S. Supreme Court in 1993. She is the first Jewish woman to serve on the Supreme Court.

Justice Ginsburg grew up in Brooklyn, New York, attended public school, and was confirmed at the East Midwood Jewish Center. On the wall of her court chambers, she has posted the Torah's teaching, "Justice, justice shall you pursue" (Deuteronomy 16:20).

Ruth Bader Ginsburg

In 1996, Justice Ginsburg wrote, "I am a judge born, raised, and proud of being a Jew. The demand for justice runs through the entirety of the Jewish tradition. I hope, in my years on the bench of the Supreme Court of the United States, I will have the strength and the courage to remain constant in the service of that demand."

Justice Ginsburg described how Jewish tradition and values have inspired her as a judge. Describe two Jewish values that influence you as a student and why.

1. _____

2. _____

Describe two Jewish values that influence you as a friend and why.

1. _____

2. _____

Go To (http://www.TheJewishProphets.com ▼

CHAPTER **6** Isaiah:

Righteous Spirit of Worship

Jerusalem is cloaked in darkness. Neighbor oppresses neighbor, the young taunt the elderly, and the wealthy mock the widowed and the orphaned.

I look up from the night and see God seated on a high and regal throne, dressed in billowing robes that fill the Temple with light. Seraphim—six-winged angels—stand in attendance, calling to one another: "Kadosh, kadosh, kadosh. Holy, holy, holy is Adonai of the heavenly legions. The whole earth is full of God's glory."

Awed and humbled, I confess that I have sinned and live among a people who have sinned. Using a pair of tongs, one of the seraphim scoops up a red-hot coal from the Temple's great altar. He brushes it lightly over my lips and declares, "Your guilt is gone and your sins forgiven."

"Who will I send? Who will accept my mission?" asks God.

And I answer with all my heart and soul, "Hineni. Here I am. Send me!"

—based on Isaiah 1 – 6

PROPHET'S PROFILE: ISAIAH

BEGINNINGS:

- Born about 765 BCE in Jerusalem.
- Hebrew Name: Yeshayahu, meaning "God will save."

PERSONAL:

- Aristocratic Roots: Born to an upper-class family; tradition teaches that Isaiah's uncle was King Amaziah; Isaiah was an advisor to Kings Hezekiah and Ahaz and may have been a Temple priest.
- Called to prophesy in his mid-twenties; preached in the southern kingdom of Judah during the reigns of four kings: Uzziah, Jotham, Ahaz, and Hezekiah.

POSTS: LOAD

Who was Isaiah?

Favorite Song: "Lo Yisa Goy El Goy Herev" ("Nation Shall not Raise Sword against Nation," Isaiah 2:4).

Most Amazing Vision: Wolves living peacefully with lambs (Isaiah 11:6).

Favorite Quotation: "'I am the first and I am the last. There is no God other than Me" (Isaiah 44:6).

Major Contribution: Taught that the godly voice of justice and mercy must rule over all nations.

Go To (http://www.TheJewishProphets.com ▼)

The Kedushah, or Holiness prayer, is the third blessing in the Amidah. It includes the words of the seraphim who sing of God's holiness in Isaiah 6:3, "Holy, holy, holy is Adonai of the heavenly legions. The whole earth is full of God's glory." One tradition is to rise up on our toes three times as we say *"Kadosh, kadosh, kadosh,"* as if we are reaching out to God.

Jumping for Justice

Who jumps at the chance to become a prophet? After all, it's hard work for no pay, and a lot of people get upset with you. Is that a job *you* would run after? Moses was the greatest of the prophets and even *he* had lots of questions. According to the midrash, he waited more than a week before accepting his mission (*Exodus Rabbah* 3:14).

But Isaiah doesn't hesitate, not even for a moment. Despite his sense that Jerusalem is covered in darkness, Isaiah is hopeful. He is eager to speak out in the name of justice and mercy. Determined to make a difference, when his chance comes, Isaiah grabs it and runs!

Early morning crowds wander through Jerusalem's open-air market amid the high-pitched bleat of camels and the bark of merchants promoting their wares. A blur of color fills the packed stalls—crimson red wool lies next to pure white fleece, deep purple grapes spill onto plump dates, and bulging sacks of golden wheat gently nudge pots of honey and vats of olive oil.

Isaiah, a tall, slender man in his twenties, carries a heavy leather satchel over his left shoulder and walks with his young son She'ar-yashuv on his right. The boy's eyes widen at the spectacle before them; the father's eyes narrow. Crafty merchants gossip and fill gourds with watered-down wine to be sold for Shabbat blessings, potters mask fine cracks in their bowls with strands of warm wax, and farmers slyly tip their scales, overcharging for grain.

Orphans and widows go unheeded as they beg for food and justice, and, only a stone's throw from the market, Temple sacrifices are offered by those who worship idols in the privacy of their home.

Slowly raising his arms, Isaiah prophesies to the crowd: "Oh, sinful nation, your hands are bloodied! Wash yourselves clean! Your rulers are scoundrels and thieves. Your animal sacrifices and empty rituals fill God with loathing. For what Adonai desires most of all is that you do what is right and just. Help those who are wronged. Uphold the rights of the orphaned. Defend the widow."

Throughout the prophecy, She'ar-yashuv remains firmly at his father's side. Other children might have become restless or pulled away. But She'ar-yashuv is no ordinary child. He is part of the prophecy. His name—which means "a remnant will return"—is the symbol of hope that although Jerusalem will fall, a small core of people will survive and rebuild the land.

—inspired by Isaiah 1, Proverbs 21: 3

What Do You Think?

In contrast to Amos, who came from a humble, rural background, Isaiah was born into an upper-class family in Jerusalem. Do you think this made it easier, as challenging, or more difficult for him to speak up and confront the people of Judah? Why?

_____

_____

THE RESPONSIBILITY TO CONFRONT WRONGDOERS

Just as the prophets confronted wrongdoers, the Torah instructs us that we, too, must let others know when they have made mistakes (Leviticus 19:17). This includes speaking up when people are hurtful to others—for example, by gossiping or by playing too aggressively on the sports field. It also includes speaking up when people are hurtful to themselves—for example, by riding a bike without a helmet or diving into a shallow pool. The Torah refers to this responsibility as *tocheiḥah*, meaning "rebuke."

According to the sage Maimonides, when we confront someone for doing wrong, it should not be done with the intention of shaming the person. Instead, it should be:

• done for the wrongdoer's own good;

• done privately, not in public; and

• expressed with concern for the wrongdoer.

The mitzvah that immediately follows the Torah's teaching to confront wrongdoers is: "Love your neighbor as yourself" (Leviticus 19:18). What connection could there be between loving your neighbor and confronting that person about his or her wrongdoing?

_____

_____

Would you want your neighbor to do the same for you? Why or why not?

_____

_____

For Isaiah, a religious Jew is a Jew who cares for those who are vulnerable—the orphaned, widowed, poor, ill, oppressed, and elderly.

How would you describe a religious Jew? What qualities and behaviors do you think are characteristic of such a person?

Isaiah spoke of Temple rites and religious fasts as "empty rituals," not because they were unimportant to him but because he believed that *righteous,* or sincere, worship of God leads to just and merciful behavior. He believed that it is hypocritical to faithfully perform religious rituals but disregard God's just and merciful laws.

His passion for the righteous worship of God continues to ring in our ears as we fast and read the *haftarah,* the portion from the Prophets, on Yom Kippur morning: "'This is the fast that I desire,' said God… 'to let the oppressed go free… to share your bread with the hungry, to take those who are poverty-stricken into your home… and to be attentive to your family'" (Isaiah 58:6 – 7).

What Do You Think?

How can the rituals of fasting and praying on Yom Kippur inspire people to become more kind and just? How might observing the rituals of Shabbat motivate someone to become more peace loving? How would you define "righteous worship"?

WE ALL MAKE MISTAKES

Jewish tradition teaches that—like Isaiah, who told God, "I confess that I have sinned"—we must take responsibility for our own mistakes in addition to confronting others for theirs. Taking responsibility can help us improve our behavior so that we feel better about ourselves. How might it also help us become more tolerant and less self-righteous, better able to confront others with compassion when they make mistakes?

_____

_____

_____

_____

Why might it be appropriate to comfort people after rebuking them? Why might showing compassion and forgiveness encourage them to improve? How might you respond to such compassion and forgiveness when you make mistakes?

Sometimes, rather than rebuking people who have made a mistake, we may put them in the "doghouse" by not speaking to them. Why might doing so feel good in the short run but be harmful in the long run? How can you help yourself when you have the impulse to put someone in the doghouse?

There are sixty-six chapters in the Book of Isaiah. Like the biblical text, this chapter of *The Prophets: Speaking Out for Justice* is written as though one person is the subject of the text. However, most scholars agree that the Book of Isaiah was written by or about several different prophets in different time periods. Many divide the book this way:

Chapters 1 to 39 were written by a prophet whom scholars call First Isaiah. He prophesied from about 740 to 688 BCE, during the period when the Assyrians conquered the kingdom of Israel and threatened to destroy the kingdom of Judah. He criticized the Judeans for their lack of faith in God and their unethical behavior. He also gave them hope that better times would come.

Chapters 40 to 55 were written by an anonymous prophet whom scholars call Second Isaiah. He lived in Babylonia (modern-day Iraq) after the Babylonians conquered Judah in 586 BCE and forced out, or exiled, many Judeans to Babylonia. Second Isaiah's message is one of comfort. He tells the exiles that they have been conquered and exiled because of their sinful behavior and that they will be returned to their homeland if they repent.

Chapters 56 to 66 were written by an anonymous prophet whom scholars call Third Isaiah. He prophesied in Jerusalem about one hundred years after the Jews returned from Babylonia to the Land of Israel, from about 440 to 420 BCE. His message was one of great hope.

Comforting Those Far from Home

Like Amos before him, Isaiah failed to inspire true faith and repentance in his people. And like the kingdom of Israel, Judah was destroyed and many of its citizens forced into exile. Yet Isaiah believed that his mission as a prophet was not over, so he, too, went into exile.

After more than half a century in Babylonia, the exiles' dream of redemption—forgiveness and freedom—was about to come true. King Cyrus of Persia appeared ready to conquer Babylonia and let the Jews return to their homeland.

Excited, Isaiah prophesied that Cyrus's victory would be a sign that God was ready to forgive the exiles. He also prophesied that God is the source of the Jewish people's strength and that the Covenant commits us to working for a just world.

> The Everlasting God, Adonai,
> Creator of the ends of the earth,
> Neither grows faint nor exhausted....
> God gives strength to the weary,
> Renewing those whose power has been lost....
> Adonai has called you in the name of justice....
> Has created you and appointed you
> A people of the Covenant, a light to the nations.
> Opening eyes that cannot see....
> Rescuing the imprisoned
> And those who sit in darkness.
> —Isaiah 40:28 – 29, 42:6 – 7

Have you ever been far from home, for example at camp, or moved to a new neighborhood or attended a new school? What did it feel like the first few days or weeks? Who cheered you up when you felt blue? What did the person say or do that helped the most?

Isaiah makes his way through the winding streets of Babylon toward the Euphrates River. As he nears the riverbank, the prophet sees the homesick exiles dressed in sackcloth and ashes, weeping and wailing, "Adonai, God of our ancestors, we repent and beg of You, do not abandon us. Do not forget us."

In Judah, Isaiah had criticized the people for their faithless and immoral ways. Now, standing on the shores of Babylonia's capital, witnessing their suffering and repentance, he yearns to comfort and inspire them with hope. He wants to tell them that God will soon end their captivity.

—based on Psalm 137 and Isaiah 40:27

LONGING FOR ISRAEL

Jewish longing to return to the Land of Israel—Eretz Yisrael—began with the exiles of Babylonia. The Book of Psalms expresses their grief: "If I forget you, O Jerusalem, let my right hand wither; let my tongue stick to the roof of my mouth if I cease to think of you, if I do not keep Jerusalem in my memory even in my happiest hour" (Psalms 137:5 – 6).

After the Second Temple was destroyed in 70 CE, Jews prayed for the rebuilding of Jerusalem. Over the centuries, we recited such prayers at Passover seders; on the fast of Tisha B'Av, which commemorates the Temple's destruction; at the end of Yom Kippur; and three times a day when we recite the Amidah.

Most Jews understood these prayers as an appeal for the speedy coming of the Messiah, whom Isaiah describes as the one who will "…gather the exiled of Israel and assemble the dispersed of Judah from the four corners of the earth" (Isaiah 11:12). But in the late 1800s, a small group of Jews committed their lives to turning our people's dream of Jewish resettlement in Eretz Yisrael into a reality. They became known as Zionists.

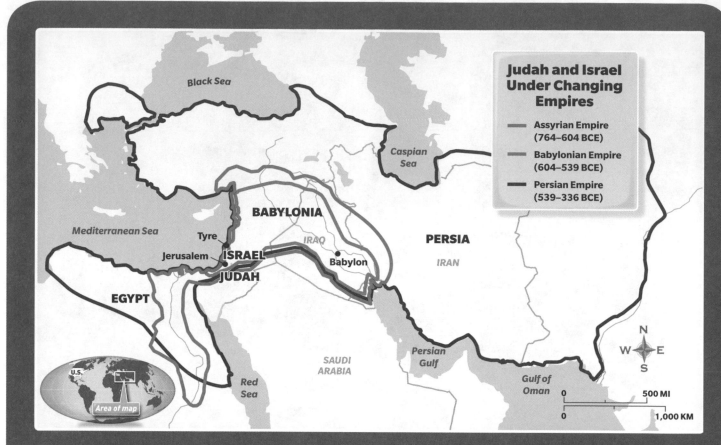

Black Sea

Caspian Sea

Mediterranean Sea

BABYLONIA

Tyre

IRAQ

PERSIA

IRAN

Jerusalem ISRAEL

Babylon

JUDAH

EGYPT

SAUDI ARABIA

Persian Gulf

Red Sea

Gulf of Oman

U.S.

Area of map

N W E S

0   500 MI

0   1,000 KM

When the northern kingdom of Israel fell to Assyria in 722 BCE and, later on, when the southern kingdom of Judah was conquered by the Babylonians in 586 BCE, many Israelites were exiled to what is now modern-day Iraq and Iran.

Isaiah encouraged the exiles saying, "Be comforted my people…. God has declared that your punishment [exile] is over, your sins forgiven…."

Historical Note

The Fall of Judah

The kingdom of Judah was conquered by the Babylonians in 586 BCE. Jerusalem and the Temple burned to the ground, and many Judeans were exiled to Babylonia. Having lost their land, their Temple, and their leaders, our ancestors had no place to farm or worship God and no one to lead them. The impoverished people of Judah and the devastated exiles were like homeless orphans.

Isaiah's Vision of a Better World

As a prophet, Isaiah wanted to do more than just comfort people and inspire them to live better lives. He also wanted to help them imagine what the world would be like—how *all* creatures would benefit—if everyone worshipped God by pursuing peace and justice.

Think about it. When you help on a project, like collecting toys for the needy or money for an animal shelter, how can your efforts not only improve the lives of those you help but also enrich your own? What would it be like if everyone pitched in? Who would benefit? How?

Isaiah used poetic language to describe his vision of the world our people can help create:

> …Godly teachings will come forth from Zion,
> The word of Adonai from Jerusalem.
> So that God will judge among nations
> And counsel the many peoples.
> They shall beat their swords into plowshares
> And their spears into pruning hooks.
> Nation shall not raise sword against nation;
> Never again will they know war…
> The wolf shall live with the lamb,
> And the leopard shall lie down
> With the kid….
>
> —Isaiah 2:3 – 4, 11:6

Sometimes in our dissatisfaction or disappointment in the world around us it is tempting to focus only on what is wrong, forgetting that there is also good and that we can work to make things better. Similarly, in our desire for dramatic improvements, we might not appreciate the value of small gains.

How do you think our individual efforts to make peace with friends and family can contribute to peace in our community?

SKILLS FOR A PEACEFUL WORLD

List three people you think of as peacemakers. They can be world-renowned, local, or even family members.

_____

_____

_____

What skills or character traits do they share that make them so good at making peace?

_____

_____

_____

GOD OF ALL THE EARTH

In Isaiah's time most people believed that each nation had its own gods. In contrast, Isaiah taught that there is only one God of Israel and that God rules over the *entire world:* "...The one who has set you free is the Holy One of Israel, who is called 'God of all the Earth'.... My Temple shall be called a house of prayer for all peoples" (Isaiah 54:5, 56:7). Isaiah's vision of a better world was one in which *all* people—Jew and non-Jew alike—worship God by showing compassion and pursuing justice and peace.

The Ten Commandments instructed the Israelites: "You shall have no other gods but Me" (Exodus 20:3). Isaiah prophesied: "... There is no God other than Me" (Isaiah 44:6).

What is the difference between these two teachings?

_____

_____

What do these two teachings tell you about how the Israelites' thinking might have changed from the time of Moses to the time of Isaiah?

_____

_____

A prophet's gift is to see flaws and shortcomings while still imagining a better world. Prophets look at themselves and their community, at their friends and even their foes, and say, "There is something much better than what we are doing. Let us dream big and figure out how to make those dreams come true. We may have failed yesterday, and we need not succeed by tomorrow, but we must try our best today."

Isaiah knew that wolves and lambs—the powerful and defenseless among us—have much work to do before peace and justice reign throughout the world. Yet he dared to imagine that we not only *can* but *will* succeed in creating that world.

Martin Luther King, Jr., wove one of Isaiah's visions of the time when all people will serve the God of justice into his most famous speech. On August 28, 1963, he said: "I have a dream that one day every valley shall be exalted, and every hill and mountain shall be made low, the rough places will be made plain, and the crooked places will be made straight; and the glory of the Lord shall be revealed and all flesh shall see it together" (based on Isaiah 40:4 – 5).

Theodor Herzl

In 1894, Theodor Herzl (1860 – 1904), an Austrian-Jewish journalist, was in Paris when Captain Alfred Dreyfus, a French Jew, was unfairly convicted of spying. On January 5, 1895, Herzl listened in horror as the crowd of twenty thousand shouted, "Death to the traitor! Death to the Jews!" Responding to this injustice, Herzl committed the rest of his life to pursuing justice for the Jewish people. He published a book called *The Jewish State*. His message: the unjust treatment of the Jews would end only when they moved from Europe to a land of their own.

Theodor Herzl (standing left of center) addressing the First Zionist Congress

On August 29, 1897, Herzl held the First Zionist Congress in Basel, Switzerland. It was the first of many accomplishments. Working tirelessly to found a Jewish state, Herzl eventually became known as "the father of Zionism."

After almost two thousand years without a Jewish state, the modern State of Israel was finally established in 1948. Although Herzl did not live to see his dream come true, like Isaiah, he was a courageous and powerful speaker who spoke up for justice and the future of the Jewish people.

Herzl is known for saying: "If you will it, it is no dream." What do you think he meant?

_____

_____

The ancient rabbis teach that Deuteronomy 16:20—"Justice, justice shall you pursue"— includes the word "justice" twice to inspire us to pursue justice both for others and for ourselves. Why are both forms of justice important?

_____

_____

Go To | http://www.TheJewishProphets.com ▼

CHAPTER **7** Jeremiah:
Persistent Voice of Teshuvah

It's a fact, I don't fit in and I never did. Even when I was young, no matter how hard I tried, I wasn't like the other kids. Dressing, talking, and joking around like them only made me feel like a phony. I finally accepted, that's not who I am. I don't know why, but I'm different.

Then, one day everything started to make sense. The voice of Adonai came to me saying, "Before you were born, I set you apart, appointing you as a prophet to the nations."

"A prophet?" I sputtered. "This must be a mistake. I'm just a kid."

"Don't say that you're just a child," God insisted. "For wherever I send you, you must go, and whatever I command you to say, you must speak." Then the Voice softened. "Don't be afraid, Jeremiah, for I am with you and will make you safe."

Reaching out, God touched my lips and continued, "I put My words in your mouth. On this day I have appointed you to preach to nations and kingdoms, to uproot and to pull down, to destroy and to root out, but also to build and to plant."

My first thought was, "I'm doomed. I'll be lonelier than ever, a social disaster." But as I listened to the Voice, I set aside my fears. Slowly, I accepted that—for better or worse—I was destined to be a prophet.

—based on Jeremiah 1:4 – 10

PROPHET'S PROFILE: JEREMIAH

BEGINNINGS:

- Born about 640 BCE in Anatot, a town just north of Jerusalem.
- Hebrew Name: Yirmeyahu, meaning "God will uplift."

PERSONAL:

- Aristocratic Roots: Born to a family of religious leaders, descendants of King David's high priest, Aviatar; Jeremiah was a priest as well as a prophet.
- Marital Status: Never married.
- Jeremiah served as a prophet for more than forty years, from 627 BCE to about 586 BCE, during a period of political and social turmoil.

POSTS:

LOAD

Who was Jeremiah?

Rap Sheet: Jeremiah was jailed twice because of his religious and political views.

Biggest Embarrassment: "…I am a constant laughingstock. Everyone mocks me" (Jeremiah 20:7).

Language Legacy: The English word *jeremiad* means "prolonged lament or complaint."

Favorite Quotation: "You will call Me and come and pray to Me; I will give heed to you. You will seek Me and find Me, if only you search for Me with all your heart. And I will allow Myself to be found by you, says Adonai…" (Jeremiah 29:12 – 14).

Major Contribution: Taught that the Torah, not the Temple, is the foundation of Judaism. This created the basis for the Israelite religion and Jewish survival not only in Israel but also outside of Israel, in the Diaspora.

Go To 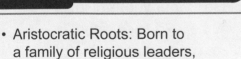 http://www.TheJewishProphets.com ▼

HELP! I CAN'T STOP MYSELF!

Despite the heartbreak and unhappiness that prophecy frequently brought Jeremiah, he could not resist his desire to speak up for truth and justice.

> I thought, "I will not mention God. I will no longer speak God's name."
>
> But God's word was like a raging fire burning in my heart.
>
> Shut up in my bones;
>
> I could not hold it in.
>
> —Jeremiah 20:9

Is there something that you believe in so deeply that you are bursting to share your ideas and beliefs with others? If so, why do you care so much? If not, do you wish that you did believe in something that deeply?

_____

_____

Kids Have What It Takes

Like Samuel, Jeremiah was about your age when he was called to prophecy. But unlike Samuel, Jeremiah pushed back, concerned that it was too big a job for a kid.

Had you been in Jeremiah's shoes might you also have felt too young to be a prophet? Might you have worried that speaking up would make you a social outcast? Or would you have been more like Samuel who seemed cool and calm about being called to prophecy?

In a midrash, our sages tell us that Jeremiah complained to God, "Was there ever a prophet whom Your people did not mistreat? They mocked Elijah, calling him 'the hairy one' [2 Kings 1:8] and nicknamed his successor, Elisha, 'baldy' [2 Kings 2:23]. They even threatened to stone the greatest prophet, Moses [Numbers 14:10]. I'm so young, Adonai, without experience and not yet wise in the ways of the world. Please, don't put such a heavy a burden on me."

"I chose you for this difficult task *because* you are young," explained God. "Your youthful innocence and trust will help you be bold and daring." (P'sikta Rabbati 26; Leviticus Rabbah 10:2).

How can you and your friends strengthen each other and work together like a team of modern-day prophets to help make your school a kinder, more welcoming, and tolerant place for all students?

How do you think innocence and trust can be sources of strength? What might be challenging for a young prophet who is asked to speak up for justice? **What traits do you have that could help make you a strong prophet?**

Despite his doubts, Jeremiah's confidence grew. He came to believe that he had both the *ability* and the *responsibility* to accept God's mission. He spoke with loyalty and dedication to God and to the kingdom of Judah, often sacrificing his personal happiness for the welfare of those he rebuked.

Jeremiah Puts His Life on the Line

Jeremiah made enemies wherever he went. Most people seemed not to like him—from the idol-worshipping citizens of Judah to the corrupt priests, from the false prophets who served the god Baal to the weak kings of Judah. The problem? Few wanted to hear that immoral behaviors, such as greed and corruption, were destroying the kingdom. Few wanted to take responsibility or repent. Yet that's exactly what Jeremiah demanded of Judah, and he would not be silenced.

The prophet began to push his luck. He delivered a controversial message, known as the Temple Sermon, at the gates of the Temple in Jerusalem. In God's name Jeremiah preached:

> …Improve your ways and your actions, and I will let you live in this place. Don't put your trust in lies and say, "The Temple of Adonai, the Temple of Adonai! This is God's Temple [and it will save us no matter how we behave]." No, if you truly improve your ways and your actions; if you are

just… and do not shed innocent blood in this place; if you do not follow other gods… only then will I let you live in this place for all time, in the land that I gave to your ancestors.

—Jeremiah 7:3 – 7

The worshippers gasped. Jeremiah had said that God's word—not the Temple—was the true foundation of their religion. He claimed that ritual

As God commanded, the prophet returned to the Temple and continued to preach his controversial message. This time it was more than his audience could bear. Seizing Jeremiah and pinning him to the ground, the enraged crowd shouted, "How dare you speak in the name of God saying that the Temple will be destroyed and Jerusalem made desolate and cursed?"

When word of Jeremiah's prophesies reached the king's palace, officials were quickly dispatched to put the prophet on trial. "Death to the traitor! Death to the one whose prophesies defame our city," his accusers cried.

Speaking in his own defense, Jeremiah swore that he had only spoken God's truth. Urging the people to change their ways, he said, "You have a choice. Heed Adonai by repenting so that your punishment will be withdrawn."

Fortunately, justice was done and Jeremiah was set free. Moved by his speech, his accusers concluded, "This man does not deserve to die for he has truly spoken in God's name."

—based on Jeremiah 26:8 – 16

worship alone would not save them. They also had to live ethical lives. The Temple priests and false prophets must have been outraged—or scared. Jeremiah was undermining their authority, casting doubt on their claim that it was the Temple that assured Jerusalem's safety.

As his audience became more agitated, Jeremiah upped his emotional pitch. If the people of Judah did not repent, he threatened, "…God's anger and God's fury will be poured out upon this place…. It shall burn and not be quenched" (Jeremiah 7:20).

A Prophet's Persistence

Never one to play it safe, when Jeremiah wasn't berating the citizens and authorities for abandoning God's laws, he was causing a ruckus about foreign affairs. Like God's other prophets, he believed that because God is the one true ruler of the world, religion governs politics. And, so, as part of his mission, Jeremiah preached a godly view of politics, one that stood for truth and justice.

Historical Note

Judah Is Vulnerable

Jeremiah lived at a time when Judah was vulnerable to invasion. The northern kingdom of Israel had been destroyed in 722 BCE by the Assyrians. In 612 BCE, after Babylonia defeated Assyria, Assyria joined forces with Egypt against Babylonia. The small kingdom of Judah was now sandwiched between two competing superpowers: Egypt in the southwest and Babylonia in the northeast.

Of the five kings who reigned in succession during Jeremiah's mission as a prophet, only the first, Josiah, worked to bring about religious reforms. Like Jeremiah, Josiah also supported Babylonia over Egypt. He died in Meggido in 609 BCE, battling the Egyptian pharaoh, Necho II. This painting illustrates Josiah's effort to bring down the idols in Jerusalem.

Let's Make a Midrash

Write a short midrash or create a drawing that portrays Jeremiah as he awaited the verdict at his trial. Before you begin, imagine that you are in Jeremiah's position. What might you be feeling and thinking as you await the judgment of others?

_____

_____

_____

_____

_____

_____

_____

_____

_____

_____

_____

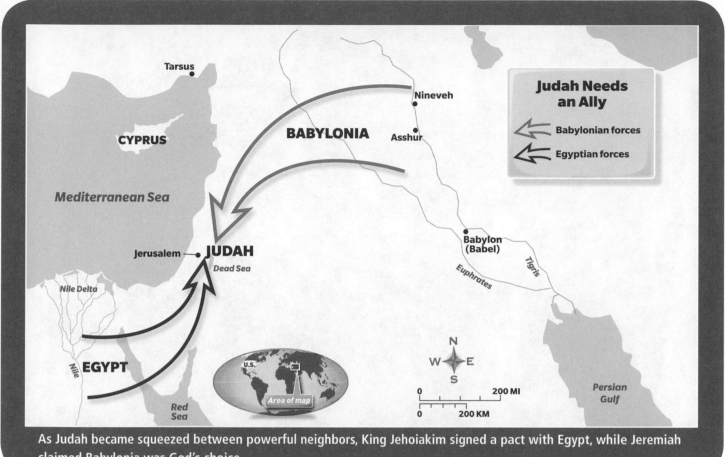

As Judah became squeezed between powerful neighbors, King Jehoiakim signed a pact with Egypt, while Jeremiah claimed Babylonia was God's choice.

Dwarfed by its large and powerful neighbors, Judah needed a strong ally—Egypt or Babylonia. King Jehoiakim chose to sign a defense pact with Egypt. Not satisfied with proclaiming that the alliance was destined to fail, Jeremiah further infuriated the authorities by arguing in favor of an alliance with Babylonia, claiming that Babylonia was God's preferred choice.

Having challenged the king's authority, the prophet's life was now under constant threat. So he went into hiding. But that didn't stop Jeremiah from speaking out. It just forced him to become more creative in how he did it.

Exhausted, the prophet shifted his weight from one foot to the other, cleared his throat, and continued dictating. Baruch ben Neriah sat at his side meticulously writing each word on parchment. A skilled scribe and a loyal partner, Baruch was committed to recording all of Jeremiah's sermons and speeches. He also agreed to read them in public on behalf of the fugitive prophet.

Baruch read the completed scroll at the Temple. When word of this reached the princes of the land they demanded that he read it to them, too. Impressed, they took the scroll and brought it before the king.

It was a cold day. Two fires blazed. One burned brightly in the hearth before King Jehoiakim; the second raged deep within him. As each section of the scroll was read, the king cut it out with a knife and threw it into the fire before him until the entire scroll was turned to ash. Then Jehoiakim ordered the arrest of Jeremiah and Baruch, but they could not be found.

A less persistent leader might have given into fear or self-pity. But Jeremiah remained determined to speak God's truth and save Judah. So, with Baruch's help, he created a second, more complete scroll and continued to pursue his mission.

—based on Jeremiah 36

What character traits and beliefs do you think Baruch shared with Jeremiah? Why?

Despite Jeremiah's best efforts, his godly message was largely ignored. In addition, he suffered the indignation of being labeled a traitor for preaching what was true and good. Eventually, Jeremiah was imprisoned by yet another king, Zedekiah, then kidnapped and forced out of Judah into Egypt. But somehow the scorned prophet kept his faith in God and his people, even after the Temple and Jerusalem were destroyed.

Success or Failure?

Was Jeremiah a success or a failure as a prophet?

On the one hand, he was not able to persuade the kingdom of Judah to accept God's teachings. On the other hand, by recording his prophecies, Jeremiah was able to reach out to future generations, urging them to make *teshuvah*—to repent—and improve. To this day, he reminds us that we have a choice, that rather than ignoring or bemoaning our mistakes, we can take responsibility for them and work to do better.

Jeremiah does not ask any one of us to save the world. He does, however, ask each of us to do our part to improve it. "You are not expected to finish the job, but you are not free to quit" (*Pirkei Avot* 2:21). He urges us to think about what we contribute and how we can do better. And he encourages us to take one small step at a time and invite others to join in.

Are you concerned, as Jeremiah was when he was your age, that this is "too big a job for a kid," or do you believe that as a young person there is much you can do to improve the world?

Prayer Connection

Me or Us?

Jeremiah took on many physical and emotional challenges. In need of strength and healing, he reached out to God, praying, "Heal me, Adonai and I will be healed; save me and I will be saved; for You are my glory" (Jeremiah 17:14).

The weekday Amidah prayer includes a blessing for healing that is based on this verse but, because the prayer is recited in community, the words "me," "I," and "my" are changed to "us," "we," and "our." Therefore, the Amidah says, "Heal us, Adonai and we will be healed; save us and we will be saved; for You are our glory."

Read the blessing in both the personal ("me," "I," and "my") and communal ("us," "we," and "our") forms. Which form speaks more powerfully to you?

The Destruction of Judah

In 597 BCE, the Babylonian king, Nebuchadnezzar, swept into Judah. He forced the king of Judah as well as its leading citizens into exile. In addition, he levied heavy taxes on the remaining population. When Judah rebelled a few years later, the Babylonian army attacked Jerusalem. In the summer of 586 BCE, Jerusalem and the Temple were burned to the ground.

So, was Jeremiah a success or a failure?

If we ignore his message and hope that someone else takes responsibility for making this a kinder, more just, and peaceful world then, yes, he failed.

But if we use his words to inspire us to become our best selves and to do our part in making things right, then there can be no doubt that Jeremiah's spirit lives on and he succeeded.

As we learn more about Judaism and pursue justice, we may have questions about why life sometimes seems unfair. Jeremiah certainly did. He wondered why the wicked often prosper, and why those who lie may go unpunished. But our doubts, like the prophet's, need not discourage us from doing what we know is right.

Nathan Sharansky

Natan Sharansky

Natan Sharansky was born in 1948 in the former Soviet Union. As a child he loved chess and mathematics and was gifted in both. In 1977, he was falsely charged with spying for the United States and imprisoned by the Communist government. However, the real reason for his arrest was his effort to help other Soviet Jews who—like him—had been refused the right to immigrate to Israel.

In his autobiography *Fear No Evil*, Sharansky explained that although the Communist system tried to break his spirit, Jewish tradition inspired him to persist in his fight for truth and justice. In 1986, after nine years of imprisonment, he was permitted to immigrate to Israel.

Sharansky held several ministerial positions in the Israeli government, including minister of industry and trade (1996–1999) and minister of the interior (1999–2000). After resigning from the Knesset in 2006, he has continued to commit his life to the welfare of the Jewish people; for example, by working as chairman of the Jewish Agency for Israel.

In what ways was Sharansky similar to Jeremiah? In what ways was he different?

Similar: _____

_____

Different: _____

_____

Go To | http://www.TheJewishProphets.com ▼

8 Jonah:

Runaway Messenger of Mercy

The great fish swooped down and swallowed Jonah ben Amittai. He landed in its belly.

Yet another snag in Jonah's plan! When Adonai's word first came to him saying, "Arise and go to Nineveh, the great city, and speak out against it because of the people's wrongdoing," Jonah hoped that he might flee from God. So he headed down to the port city of Jaffa and boarded a ship for Tarshish instead. But God pursued him, sending a great wind and a raging storm, whose fierceness threatened to destroy the craft and every creature on it.

Unshaken, Jonah calmly went below deck and fell asleep, disregarding the trembling crew, who watched as wave after wave of turbulent water battered and flooded their ship. Terrified, each sailor cried out to his own god. But the storm raged on. The seamen then hurled their cargo overboard to lighten the ship's burden. Those efforts were futile, too. Desperate, the crew cast lots to learn who had brought such evil upon them.

The lot fell on Jonah, who had been awakened by the captain. "Cast me into the water and the sea will calm down, for this great storm was sent by God on my account," he told the sailors. Fearing Adonai, the men threw Jonah overboard, which is how he met the great fish.

PROPHET'S PROFILE: JONAH

BEGINNINGS:

- The Book of Jonah doesn't offer much detail about the prophet's life. But 2 Kings 14:25 says that "the prophet Jonah son of Amittai from Gat-hepher," lived in the northern kingdom of Israel
- Hebrew Name: Yonah, meaning "dove."

PERSONAL:

- Back-to-Life Buzz: According to legend, a child whom the prophet Elijah miraculously brought back to life (I Kings 17) grew up to be the prophet Jonah.
- Common Misconception: Many people think Jonah was swallowed by a whale, but the Bible describes the creature simply as a "great fish" (Jonah 2:1).

POSTS: ✉   LOAD

Who was Jonah?

Itinerary Update: Jonah went to Jaffa, an ancient port city that is now part of Tel Aviv. His plan was to flee to the city of Tarshish, which some scholars think was in Spain. Nineveh was one of the largest cities in the Assyrian Empire, located in the area of modern-day Iraq.

Superstition: Among sailors the term "Jonah" refers to a sailor or passenger who may bring bad luck and endanger the ship.

Greatest Embarrassment: Jonah fooled himself into thinking that he could run away from God's presence.

Favorite Quotation: "Those who cling to what is false will lose [God's] bounty…" (Jonah 2:9).

Major Contribution: Jonah's story teaches that mercy is available to all people, and no one who repents sincerely can be denied it.

Go To (http://www.TheJewishProphets.com ▼)

Jonah passed three days and nights in the beast's belly. Praying with all his heart, he cried, "Out of my distress I call to Adonai." And when he said, "Deliverance is given by Adonai," God commanded the fish to spit Jonah up onto dry land.

The word of Adonai came to Jonah a second time: "Arise and go to Nineveh, the great city, and cry out My message." This time Jonah arose and went to Nineveh to prophesy for God.

—based on Jonah 1:1 – 3:3

WALK OR TALK?

Jonah was not the only prophet who resisted God's calling. Moses also resisted, arguing that he was slow of speech; Amos said that he didn't have the right training or family background; and Jeremiah complained that he was too young. But Jonah was the only prophet who turned away from God and fled without a word.

Imagine that your mother or father has asked you to do something you don't want to do. What might make you want to just walk away?

How might discussing the issue instead help the situation?

_____

_____

What would help you decide to talk rather than walk away?

_____

_____

A Surprisingly Great Story

The Book of Jonah has all the ingredients of an action-packed adventure story— a fugitive on the high seas, a raging storm, a man thrown overboard, and a country of evildoers. You couldn't ask for more. But because it's the Bible you get a *whole* lot more.

Besides being a first-rate story, this sacred text is also filled with great surprises. One is that God doesn't send Jonah on a mission to save the Israelites. Instead, Jonah is commanded to save the people of Nineveh. The fact that a nation's holy book is devoted to a story about saving a different people is startling enough, but the Ninevites weren't just any people. They were Assyrians, the *archenemies* of Israel, a cruel and corrupt people!

What sense can we make of that? Why would our tradition teach that people who want to obliterate us should be given the chance to repent and survive?

Why is the Book of Jonah, of all the books of the Prophets, the *haftarah* on the afternoon of Yom Kippur, the holiest day of the Jewish year?

And, most important, what do Jonah—a runaway prophet—and the cruel people of Nineveh have to teach us about godliness?

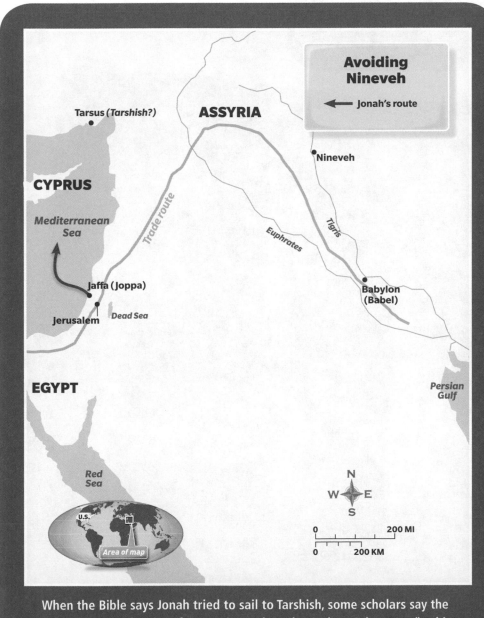

Avoiding Nineveh

← Jonah's route

Tarsus (*Tarshish?*)

ASSYRIA

Nineveh

CYPRUS

Mediterranean Sea

Trade route

Euphrates

Tigris

Jaffa (Joppa)

Babylon (Babel)

Jerusalem

Dead Sea

EGYPT

Persian Gulf

Red Sea

N W E S

U.S.

Area of map

0   200 MI
0   200 KM

When the Bible says Jonah tried to sail to Tarshish, some scholars say the reference is to the city of Tarsus, in modern-day Turkey. Others say "a ship bound for Tarshish" meant any ship equipped for a long voyage.

Prayer Connection

An Early Thanksgiving

Jonah's prayer from the depths of the sea opens with words of despair. So, you might think that he would ask for forgiveness or at least beg to be saved. But Jonah neither repents for fleeing nor pleads for his life. Instead, his prayer is like a psalm of thanksgiving. He speaks as if he already has been saved, is back on dry land, and is heading for the Temple.

You cast me… into the heart of the ocean…. Weeds wrapped around my head. I sank to the bottom of the mountains. The earth's bars closed behind me forever [like a prison]. Yet You brought my life up from the pit, O Adonai my God!… I, with great thanksgiving, will sacrifice to You [at the Temple]….
—Jonah 2:4 – 10

Why do you think Jonah thanks God in advance of being saved and promises to make a Temple sacrifice in Jerusalem? Why do you think God saves Jonah?

Understanding

How can studying the Book of Jonah with your classmates help you develop a greater understanding of its lessons? How might you use the Internet to increase your understanding?

"Nineveh will be overthrown in forty days," Jonah alerted the great city. His words were like the shrill call of a shofar that awakens the spirit. Mouths that had led the innocent astray became tight lipped and silent. Hands that had clutched at stolen goods loosened their grip. And eyes that had been blinded by envy now turned toward Jonah, eager to see.

The people believed God. Declaring a fast, they immediately covered themselves in sackcloth. And when God's word reached the king of Nineveh, he arose from his throne, removed his royal robes, covered himself with sackcloth, and sat in ashes.

Royal messengers cried throughout Nineveh: "By decree of the king and his nobles, let no human or beast taste anything! Not graze nor drink water! Let them be covered in sackcloth—every human and beast—and let the people call mightily to God. Let every one of us turn away from evil and injustice. Perhaps God will turn back from anger and repent the harsh verdict so that we do not die."

God saw how the people of Nineveh turned away from doing evil. And God repented the verdict so that they did not die.

—based on Jonah 3

Throughout the centuries, each generation has asked these questions and searched for answers that are meaningful to them. Jewish tradition now invites us to search for our own answers, raise new questions, and share our thoughts with one another. In this way, as we study Jonah's story we may discover not only a few surprises and lessons about Judaism but also about ourselves.

Repentance Wins the Day

Jonah was as good as his word. He went to Nineveh and preached God's message, which showed a lot of courage.

How might you have felt walking through enemy territory delivering news that could antagonize the population?

How do you think Jonah felt? In what ways might he have changed since the storm at sea? How might he have remained the same? Why do you think so?

The Book of Jonah is unlike other books of the Prophets. Not only doesn't it tell about the history of our people, it also doesn't offer much prophecy. The only words Jonah ever preaches are, "Nineveh will be overthrown in forty days" (Jonah 3:4).

Talk about surprises! Everything in the Book of Jonah seems topsy-turvy. First we meet a prophet who not only doesn't model godly behavior but tries to run away from God. Next we are introduced to a cruel and corrupt people who, unlike the holy nation of Israel, quickly repent and change their sinful ways. But perhaps the biggest surprise of all is that God repents. Since when does God repent—or even need to?

Let's go step by step. The truth is that Jonah isn't the only prophet to make a mistake or to disregard God's command. For example, The book of Numbers teaches that God told Moses to *order* the rock in the Sinai wilderness to produce water for the thirsty Israelites. But Moses *hit* the rock twice with his rod (Numbers 20:7 – 11).

Perhaps we sometimes expect righteous people or strong leaders, like Moses or our parents, not merely to be good or very good but to be perfect. Yet the Bible teaches that even prophets make mistakes. After all, if they were perfect they wouldn't be human and we couldn't hope to be like them.

What helps you accept that the people you love and respect aren't perfect? How can you apply that understanding to accepting yourself even as you try to become a better person?

The Bible also teaches that even the cruelest and most corrupt people, like the Ninevites, can change for the good. What a source of encouragement and hope. For if the worst among us can turn away from bad habits and behaviors, how much more likely it is that those of us who are just a little confused, a little weak, or a little foolish will succeed in developing new strengths.

The Talmud says, "It is not written that…'God saw [the people of Nineveh in] sackcloth and fasting,' but rather that 'God saw what they did, how they had turned away from their evil behavior'" (Mishnah, *Ta'anit* 2:1). Why are prayer and fasting important parts of *teshuvah?* Why are we required to also work on our behavior; for example, by being more thoughtful and kind?

Finally, we have the matter of God repenting. What can that possibly mean? To repent is to have regret and to change. Yet Jewish tradition often speaks of God as perfect and unchanging. On careful reading of the Book of Jonah we see that the text does not say that God changes. Rather it teaches that when humans change their behavior for the better, God repents plans to punish them.

What can this teach us about holding grudges versus giving others a second chance? Although, at first, it might feel easier to hold a grudge or punish others rather than forgive them, why might doing so cause greater difficulties in the long run?

Will We Listen or Turn Away?

The Book of Jonah could have concluded with the saving of the Ninevites. After all, Jonah and the Ninevites had changed their behavior for the better. End of story. Done.

Not.

The story continues because there is still unfinished business. Jonah may have followed God's command, but his heart and soul weren't in it. Perhaps like us, he needed to learn a few more lessons.

What Do You Think?

Scholars believe that the Book of Jonah was actually written sometime between 599 BCE and 300 BCE, centuries after the story takes place. This means that it was written after the Assyrians destroyed the Kingdom of Israel in 722 BCE. Why would our tradition include a story in which God sends a prophet to save the very people who would one day bring down the Israelites?

GOD'S PRAYER

Like the Book of Jonah, the Talmud is full of surprises. One big surprise is the sages' teaching that God prays. In fact, they tell us what God prays: "May it be My will that My mercy tame My anger and that My mercy may triumph over My other attributes so that I may deal with my children in compassion rather than strict justice" (Talmud, *B'rachot 7a*).

What does the prayer teach about godliness?

_____

_____

What does the prayer teach about how to treat other people?

_____

_____

Write a prayer that can inspire you to treat yourself or others better. Then write one action you can take to help fulfill the goal of your prayer.

The prayer:

_____

_____

_____

_____

The action:

_____

_____

"This is not fair!" Jonah fumed. And in his rage he prayed to God, "Please, Adonai! When I was still in Israel this is exactly what I feared. This is why I tried to flee to Tarshish. I knew you were a merciful and gracious God, slow to anger, overflowing with kindness, and forgiving of evil."

Adonai gently asked, "Are you so deeply angered?"

Old habits die hard. Jonah left the city without saying a word. He was enraged that God had forgiven the Ninevites without punishing them. In a place east of Nineveh he made a hut and sat in it, waiting to see what would become of the city. But the leafy branches that topped his hut began to whither in the blazing sun. So God provided a castor-oil plant and placed it next to Jonah. It quickly grew, its large green leaves reaching above his head, shading him. Jonah was greatly pleased.

At dawn the next day, God sent a worm that attacked the plant, leaving it to wither. Then, when the sun rose, God sent a hot east wind to blow. The heat was so intense that Jonah nearly fainted, which made him even angrier than he was before.

"You're this angry about the plant?" God asked.

"Yes," Jonah replied, "so deeply enraged that I want to die."

Then Adonai said, "You care about the castor-oil plant for which you did no work. You didn't plant it or do anything to help it grow. It just appeared overnight then died overnight. Should I not care about Nineveh, that great city in which there are more than one hundred and twenty thousand people who cannot yet distinguish their right hand from their left...."

—based on Jonah 4

Once again, we watch as Jonah walks away from God and does not repent. Yet he begrudges the Ninevites who do repent—who not only express regret for their mistakes but also become better people. Ironically, Jonah doesn't value that Nineveh is now less likely to be the enemy of Israel. Instead, he seeks strict justice, demanding severe punishment for those who have erred.

In the story God does not give up on Jonah any more than God gave up on the people of Nineveh. God speaks gently and patiently, yet firmly, to the prophet, explaining that when we give of ourselves to other creatures we are more likely to care about them. Jonah did nothing to grow or nurture the castor-oil plant. When it died he was upset for self-centered, not compassionate, reasons—he had lost the plant's shade!

The Torah teaches that God cares deeply about humans, for God created and nurtured all of humankind, placing a godly spark in each of us—friend and foe alike, the wrong-headed and the righteous, the cowardly and the courageous, the Jew and the non-Jew.

Why might this teaching help us show mercy to others? Why might it help us feel worthy of forgiveness?

It's easy to forget that although we each have different strengths and weaknesses; we are all human, all imperfect, and all in need of each other's concern and caring. Yes, the Book of Jonah teaches that it is our duty to rebuke those who err, but it also teaches that it is our duty to do so in a merciful

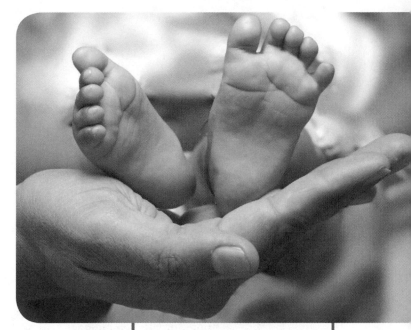

Jewish tradition sometimes speaks of God as a caring parent. How do you think the story of Jonah portrays God? With what other people or roles might you compare God?

way, encouraging improvement, helping and rooting for one another to succeed.

Why might you want to both rebuke and root for someone who has been hurtful to you? How might you do that?

The Bible doesn't tell us if Jonah ever changed his attitude and behavior. Perhaps it is because there is a bit of the prophet in each of us, and we are meant to complete the story through our own lives. Like Jonah, we each have the potential to hear the godly voice that can guide us toward repentance and mercy. And, like Jonah, we have the choice to listen or turn away.

Our tradition teaches that the gates of return to God are always open, and all who enter doing *teshuvah* are greeted with mercy and love. Every day is filled with opportunities to think about the path we are on, alter it for the better, and move forward in partnership with others.

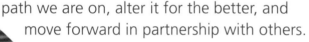

Think of a time when you made a mistake and someone responded with kindness and compassion instead of anger. How can that person's behavior be a model for you, reminding you to treat others in a patient and loving way?

Henrietta Szold

Henrietta Szold

Baltimore-born Henrietta Szold (1860 – 1945) made her first visit to the Land of Israel in 1909. Troubled by the unhealthy living conditions of the children there, Szold returned to the United States to form Hadassah, the Women's Zionist Organization of America. For the rest of her life, she worked to improve health care and education for the Jews and Arabs of Eretz Yisrael. Rather than see Jews and Arabs as enemies, she saw them as human beings in need of her skills and assistance.

Hadassah sent American-trained nurses and, later, entire medical units to the Land of Israel to combat primitive health conditions. It worked to improve maternity and infant care, and to set up training programs for nurses, as well as health clinics, and, later, hospitals.

The Hadassah University Medical Center opened in Jerusalem in 1939. Today it is considered one of the finest hospitals in the Middle East. It continues Szold's commitment to providing quality medical care to Jews and Arabs.

Szold is also known for other life-saving work. After Hitler came to power in Germany in 1933, thousands of Jewish children from Germany were sent by their parents to live in Eretz Yisrael. They were part of Youth Aliyah, a project directed by Szold to help young Jews escape the Nazis. About five thousand teenagers arrived in the Jewish homeland before World War II, and more than fifteen thousand children came after the war.

Describe two Jewish values that may have inspired Szold's concern both for Jews and for Arabs.

_____

_____

Go To http://www.TheJewishProphets.com ▼

Index

Values Index

Comfort: Isaiah

Compassion: Moses

Confidence: Amos, Elijah

Confronting/rebuking: Isaiah; Jeremiah; Jonah

Courage: Elijah

Determination: Elijah

Ethical Leadership: Moses; Samuel; Elijah

Forgiveness: Amos; Isaiah

Holiness: Isaiah

Hope: Isaiah

Humility: Amos

Justice: Moses; Amos; Isaiah; Elijah; Jeremiah

Loyalty and service to God: Samuel; Deborah;
    Elijah; Jeremiah

Mercy: Isaiah, Jonah

Peace: Amos, Isaiah

Responsibility: Moses; Amos; Isaiah, Jeremiah

Social Justice: Amos

Speaking from the heart: Hannah

Teshuvah/repentance: Jeremiah; Jonah

Thankfulness: Jonah

Truth: Jeremiah